IMAGES
of America

SISTERS OF
NOTRE DAME
OF CLEVELAND

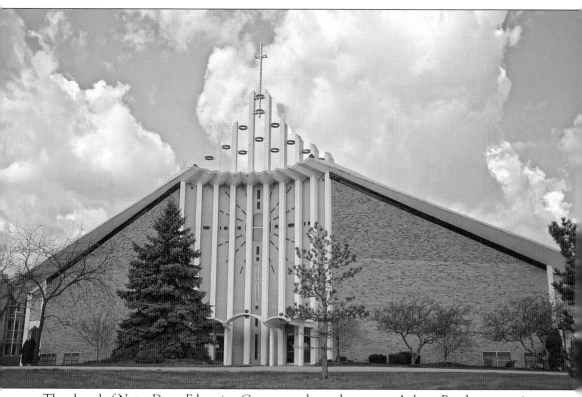

The chapel of Notre Dame Education Center stands as a beacon on Auburn Road, announcing the home of the Sisters of Notre Dame and Notre Dame Schools in Geauga County. (Sisters of Notre Dame, Chardon.)

ON THE COVER: At the National Shrine of the Immaculate Conception in Washington, DC, these sisters accompanied Regina High School's senior pilgrimage in 1979. From left to right are Srs. Mary Catherine (Patrick Brigid) O'Malley, Susan (Carlyn) Clark, Cecilia (Ranata) Liberatore, Frances Murray, Sally (Ruthanne) Huston, and Carol (Michael Paul) Dikovitsky. (Sisters of Notre Dame, Chardon.)

IMAGES
of America

SISTERS OF
NOTRE DAME
OF CLEVELAND

Jackie —
Thank you
for being friends
of SND.

Eileen Quinlan, SND

Sr Eileen Quinlan SND

ARCADIA
PUBLISHING

Published by Arcadia Publishing
Charleston, South Carolina

Printed in the United States of America

Library of Congress Control Number: 2019936584

For all general information, please contact Arcadia Publishing:
Telephone 843-853-2070
Fax 843-853-0044
E-mail sales@arcadiapublishing.com
For customer service and orders:
Toll-Free 1-888-313-2665

Visit us on the Internet at www.arcadiapublishing.com

*This book is dedicated to the Sisters of Notre Dame who lived this story,
and who will continue to proclaim God's goodness and provident care.*

CONTENTS

ACKNOWLEDGMENTS

Sr. Margaret Mary Gorman, Sr. Patricia Mary Garrahan, and Francis Piccirillo graciously gave permission, encouragement, and support for this project. I am grateful.

The well-researched works of Srs. Mary Luke Arntz, Maria Raphaelita Böckmann, Mary Jessica Karlinger, Mary Loretta Pastva, and Mary Joanne Wittenburg, as well as Sister Mary Vincentia's *Their Quiet Tread*, have been indispensable sources for the present book.

For their assistance with locating information and photographs, I am grateful to Srs. Mary Elizabeth Wood, Maria Elke Baumann, Betty Mae Bienlein, Maryann Humenik, Joan Terese Niklas, Regina Robbins, Patricia Teckman, Alice Marie Willman, and Joanne Wittenburg, and the many sisters who provided information about their ministries. I am also grateful to these people for providing information and photographs: Brian Meggitt, Cleveland Public Library; William Barrow and staff, Cleveland State University; Phil Haas and Carol Kovach, Diocese of Cleveland; Mary Kate Farrar, Gesu Parish, University Heights; Lynee Bixler, Julie Billiart Schools, Lyndhurst; Joe Prada and Judy Lewis, Metro Catholic School, Cleveland; Patricia Harding and Paula Baughn, Notre Dame College, South Euclid; Keven Krajnak, Notre Dame Schools, Chardon; Carrie Higginbotham, Margie Wilber, and Angela Sedivy, SND Mission Advancement Office, Chardon; Ann Norman and Jeff Piorkowski, Sun Newspapers; Mother Mary Louise Kane, PBVM, Watervliet, New York; Debbie Buerger, the Chapel at St. Aloysius, Cincinnati; and Michiel Verbeek, Joe Darwal, Jim Olexa, Mrs. Larry P. Brown, and Ken Kleppel and the family of Frances Meister Schmidt.

Srs. Mary Rose Falorio, Therese Dugan, Seton Schlather, Mary Quinlan, Anne Marie Robinson, and Marie Julie Bruss gave essential feedback on content, style, and mechanics at many stages of the text's development. I am grateful.

Finally, I thank the thousands of Sisters of Notre Dame whose stories are in these pages and whose witness to God's goodness and provident care continues to be a gift to all of God's people. God is good, all the time.

Images in this volume appear courtesy of the Cleveland Public Library (CPL); Cleveland Press Collection, Michael Schwartz Library, Cleveland State University (CSU); the Diocese of Cleveland (DC); Gesu Parish (GP); Julie Billiart Schools (JB); Metro Catholic School (MC); Mission Advancement Office (MA); Notre Dame–Cathedral Latin School (NDCL); Notre Dame College (NDC); Sisters of Notre Dame, Los Angeles (CA); Sisters of Notre Dame, Covington (CO); Sisters of Notre Dame, Toledo (TO); and SND Generalate Archives, Rome (SND). Unless otherwise noted, all other images appear courtesy of the Sisters of Notre Dame, Chardon.

INTRODUCTION

You may be reading this book because the Sisters of Notre Dame were your teachers in elementary school or high school, or because your mother or grandmother went to the Academy or Regina. Perhaps you've attended the Chicken Barbecue & Boutique, or worked alongside the sisters in your parish or a service agency, or one of your relatives was a sister. Whether you know them or are meeting them for the first time, this book can be a window on the life and work of the Sisters of Notre Dame of Cleveland.

Because the main ministry of the Cleveland Sisters of Notre Dame has been education, many people associate the sisters with the school buildings where they lived and taught. The first motherhouse stood near St. Peter Church at East Seventeenth Street and Superior Avenue in downtown Cleveland. Castle Ansel was the Tudor Gothic provincial house and academy on Ansel Road at East Ninety-Third Street overlooking Rockefeller Park. Now based in Geauga County's Munson Township, the sisters have been a vibrant presence since their 1874 arrival from Germany to teach the children of immigrants in parish schools in Cleveland, Toledo, and Covington, Kentucky, and in German farming communities across northern Ohio. The academic excellence of their schools led to invitations to teach in many other elementary and secondary schools, as well as their own academies. Their program to prepare young sisters as effective Catholic schoolteachers led to establishing the liberal arts–focused Notre Dame College in Cleveland. Generations have credited the Sisters of Notre Dame with the solid educational foundation for their personal and professional lives, and for lifelong friendships.

Their teaching ministry gradually brought them into more parishes and neighborhoods. From the farm communities of Lorain and Portage Counties, to the Slovak and Slovenian neighborhoods of Cleveland, to the growing cities and suburbs of Cuyahoga and Mahoning Counties, the Sisters of Notre Dame taught in schools and religious education programs, played the organ in church, and trained altar servers. As families grew to know and love the sisters, many of their daughters saw in Notre Dame a joyful and meaningful way of life, and joined the community. After only 50 years, the community of 200 immigrant German sisters had become more than 600 women of many ethnic backgrounds, spread over dozens of towns in northern and southern Ohio and northern Kentucky. In 1924, the American community was divided into three provinces, separate administrative units in Covington, Toledo, and Cleveland, each with its own provincial house, novitiate, and academy. Relationships continued to grow across the country as each province established more schools, expanding into more communities.

The Cleveland Sisters of Notre Dame established their first distant missions in 1924 in the growing Los Angeles area, and in the 1930s sent sisters to the Campus School of the Catholic University of America in Washington, DC. After World War II, the sisters accepted a school in Virginia, a hospital in Tennessee, and a mission in northern India. The Cleveland community grew to nearly 800 sisters in the mid-1960s, and by the 1970s, sisters were teaching in Virginia, North Carolina, and Florida. The need for more space for the novitiate and Notre Dame Academy led to the construction of a new provincial center and academy near Chardon, Ohio, which expanded both mission and outreach. On the Chardon campus, thousands of neighbors, friends, and family have enjoyed the annual Chicken Barbecue & Boutique, the community's main event for fund-raising—and friend-raising—since 1962. The Chardon campus is also home to Notre Dame Village, a senior living community where neighbors connect with the pre-K–12 students of Notre Dame Schools and with the liturgical and cultural life of the sisters.

Sharing their life and experience of God's goodness and provident care has been the mission of the Sisters of Notre Dame since their founding in Coesfeld, Westphalia, Prussia (now Germany) in 1850. They have most often carried out their mission through classroom education at all levels since coming to the United States in 1874. The renewal of religious life called for by Vatican Council II (1962–1965) and by the congregation's own general chapter meetings has resulted in an ever-deepening understanding of the original charism of St. Julie Billiart (1751–1816), foundress of the Sisters of Notre Dame of Namur and spiritual mother of the Coesfeld congregation, and of the Coesfeld foundresses, Hilligonde Wolbring (1828–1881) and Elisabeth Kühling (1822–1869). This spiritual rejuvenation has enriched the sisters' spirituality and ministry, and has opened new ministries through which the sisters can make God's goodness known to more people in a greater variety of circumstances.

Now, in the 21st century, the Sisters of Notre Dame in Cleveland, Covington, Los Angeles, and Toledo see themselves as "sisters without borders," vitally connected with Notre Dame around the world: in Germany, Italy, the Netherlands, England, Brazil, Peru, South Korea, China, the Philippines, Papua New Guinea, Indonesia, Vietnam, India, Mozambique, Tanzania, Kenya, and Uganda. The four US regions will reunite as a single American province in 2020. Despite the realities of fewer members and a higher median age, the Sisters of Notre Dame are nevertheless on mission, full of life, welcoming new members, ready to bring God's goodness wherever they are called to be.

In 1991, the sisters could choose to return to their baptismal name or keep their religious name. A name in parentheses indicates a sister's former religious name; for example, Sr. Mary Anne (Emeric) Blasko.

Prologue

ORIGINS

The Congregation of the Sisters of Notre Dame in Coesfeld began when two young schoolteachers, Hilligonde Wolbring and Elisabeth Kühling, and several orphan girls moved into the St. Annatal convent buildings in the spring of 1850. The associate priest of their parish, Rev. Theodor Elting, had purchased the property while negotiating to bring the Sisters of Notre Dame of Amersfoort, Netherlands, to Coesfeld to train the two teachers for religious life.

Both Wolbring and Kühling were graduates of the Royal Teacher Training College in Münster, and trained in the pedagogy of Rev. Bernard Overberg, who had revolutionized the professional preparation of both diocesan priests and the teachers of the diocese. Nearly all of the first sisters of the Coesfeld congregation were graduates of the same teacher preparation program; one of their first community decisions was to open a teacher-training school in Coesfeld to prepare young sisters to be educators in parish schools.

The Amersfoort Sisters of Our Lady who trained the Coesfeld novices owed their foundation to a Dutch Jesuit, Rev. Mathias Wolff, who brought several young women to the Ghent novitiate of the Sisters of Notre Dame de Namur in 1819. After their formation, these young sisters established a Notre Dame convent in Amersfoort in 1822. The Amersfoort sisters began with the constitutions, finalized by Julie Billiart's successor, Françoise Blin de Bourdon, in Namur in 1818.

Julie and Françoise had established the first Sisters of Notre Dame in 1804 in Amiens, France. Disagreements with the bishop of Amiens led to the transfer of the motherhouse to Namur in 1809. The Namur congregation made its first foundation in the United States in 1840, in Cincinnati, Ohio.

In 1884, Mother Maria Chrysostoma met the Notre Dame de Namur sisters in Cincinnati, who explained how the two congregations were related to Julie Billiart. Since Julie's beatification in 1906 and her 1969 canonization, the three congregations—Namur, Amersfoort, and Coesfeld—have deepened their understanding of their shared Notre Dame spirituality.

Julie Billiart (1751–1816) gathered a group of women after the French Revolution to teach girls catechism and skills for earning a living. The Sisters of Notre Dame were officially organized in 1804, and their constitutions were approved in 1818 by the bishop of Namur, a city now in Belgium, where the motherhouse was established. (SND.)

Rev. Bernard Overberg (1754–1826), a priest of the Diocese of Münster, in Westphalia, developed teaching methods focused on "the whole child," pioneered curriculum for the formal preparation of teachers, and influenced the seminary training of priests. In addition, he established a normal school in Münster in 1783 to train men as schoolteachers; in 1832, the training college for women was established in Münster.

An orphan raised by relatives in Rotterdam, Hilligonde Wolbring (1828–1889) lived in Bocholt with the family of an Overberg-trained teacher. Educated at Münster's Teacher Training College, she taught at the St. Lambert Parish school, Coesfeld, with Elisabeth Kühling. After professing vows in October 1852, Hilligonde—now Sister Maria Aloysia—continued as a teacher until the 1874 move to Cleveland.

Born in Münster, Elisabeth Kühling (1822–1869) graduated from the teacher training college and taught at St. Lambert, Coesfeld. The parish priest, Rev. Elting, rented a house where she and Hilligonde Wolbring cared for seven girls whose families could no longer support them. Elisabeth made vows in 1852 as Sister Maria Ignatia. From 1858 until her death, she trained novices in religious life as Sisters of Notre Dame.

In Coesfeld, a city in North Rhine-Westphalia chartered in 1197, St. Lambert was already a parish in the year 809, when St. Ludger preached here. The present church is a late medieval building with a bell tower dating from the mid-1600s. A treasured relic in the church is the oak and walnut crucifix, which has been venerated since 1312. In this parish, the Coesfeld Sisters of Notre Dame began.

Theodor Elting (1819–1862) studied in the Münster seminary founded by Rev. Bernard Overberg. In the spirit and work of the young teachers Hilligonde Wolbring and Elisabeth Kühling, he recognized the potential for a religious congregation devoted to the education of girls. With the bishop's permission, Reverend Elting contacted the Sisters of Our Lady in Amersfoort, Netherlands, about forming the young teachers for religious life.

These young Sisters of Our Lady of Amersfoort, Netherlands, belonged to a congregation formed by the Sisters of Notre Dame de Namur in Ghent in 1822, guided by Rev. Mathias Wolff, a Jesuit priest who saw the need for a women's congregation in the Netherlands. The Amersfoort congregation adapted the 1818 Namur constitutions. Amersfoort is about 100 miles from Münster.

Coesfeld's St. Annatal convent, built in the 15th century and abandoned since 1810, was purchased by Reverend Elting at Christmastime 1849. By fall 1850, it was home to Hilligonde Wolbring, Elisabeth Kühling, more than 30 girls, and three Dutch Sisters of Our Lady who had come to form the two young teachers as sisters. St. Annatal was the congregation's motherhouse until 1875.

This seal of the congregation of the Sisters of Notre Dame of Coesfeld, struck around 1850, bears the monogram of Mary surmounted by a cross and surrounded by 12 stars (Revelation 12:1) and images of the Sacred Hearts of Jesus and Mary. When political tensions forced the Dutch sisters' return to Amersfoort in 1855, the newly independent Coesfeld congregation elected Sr. Mary Anna Scheffer-Boichorst first superior general, 1856–1872.

After Mother Maria Chrysostoma Heck (superior general 1872–1895) met the Cincinnati Sisters of Notre Dame de Namur, connections between the congregations developed. In 2004, a spirituality conference held in Springfield, Massachusetts, marked St. Julie's 1804 foundation in Namur. In attendance were Amersfoort sisters (left), Namur's congregational leader Camilla Burns SND, and Srs. Melannie Svoboda (Chardon provincial superior), and Joanne Miller.

One

BEGINNINGS
1874–1924

The Sisters of Notre Dame left Prussia in the mid-1870s to escape the anti-Catholic legislation of the Bismarck government. Some sisters remained in the Netherlands and various German states, but most sailed to America, establishing the congregation's headquarters first in Covington, from 1875 to 1878, and then in Cleveland until 1888. Working among immigrants, the sisters quickly adapted to language, climate, and culture in Ohio and Kentucky. They maintained the structure of their religious life but learned to let go of nonessentials, always focusing on their mission: bringing the Gospel wherever God led them.

At first, they did what they had done in Prussia, teaching in German parish schools and caring for orphans. But their understanding of their mission quickly expanded as they were invited to Irish, Slovak, Bohemian, and Lithuanian parishes, both rural and urban. Far-off missions in Iowa and Pennsylvania ended quickly, letting the community focus its energies in Ohio.

When conditions in Prussia improved, the motherhouse was reestablished in Mülhausen, Germany, in 1888, and the community in America began further adaptations. As American women entered the novitiate, Notre Dame became an English-speaking community with German customs. The sisters responded to America's changing educational needs by opening secondary schools, establishing a liberal arts college for women, and meeting state teacher certification requirements. The Overberg educational legacy, part of the sisters' formation for religious life, was integrated into Ohio's preprofessional standards. Their reputation for teaching excellence increased the demand for Sisters of Notre Dame in schools throughout the region.

The sisters sank roots in their new country by building imposing convents and academies in Cleveland, Toledo, and Covington. After 1888, Cleveland was the provincial center, with Covington and Toledo as district centers. Significant growth in the American community—from 200 sisters to more than 600 in less than 50 years—resulted in the 1924 decision to establish the three centers as individual provinces, each with a provincial superior and novitiate. During the prosperous 1920s, the congregation in the United States was poised for still more growth.

Aboard the SS *Rhein*, superior general Mother Maria Chrysostoma and eight sisters, including foundress Sister Maria Aloysia, sailed from Bremen on June 19, 1874, landing on July 4 in New York, where they were quite surprised by the fireworks. Within three years, nearly all of the Coesfeld community—about 200 sisters—had arrived to serve in parishes near Cleveland and Toledo, Ohio, and Covington, Kentucky.

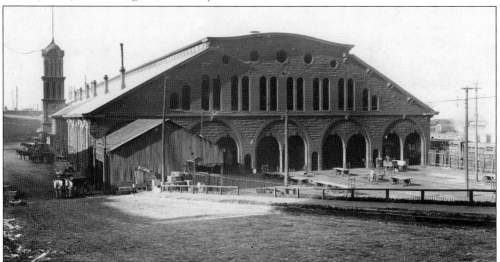

On the evening of July 6, 1874, the pioneer sisters' train journey from Hoboken, New Jersey, ended at Cleveland's Union Depot, built in 1866 at the foot of Water (West Ninth) Street on the shore of Lake Erie. Rev. Francis Westerholt, pastor of Cleveland's St. Peter Parish, met them and drove them to their house on Huntington (now East Eighteenth) Street. (CPL.)

Having left Westphalia at age 24, Francis Westerholt (1827–1896) entered Cleveland's seminary and was ordained in 1855. After serving at St. John in Delphos, Ohio, Reverend Westerholt was appointed to St. Peter Church on Superior Avenue. His friend in Coesfeld, Reverend Stuhlreyer, forwarded Mother Maria Chrysostoma's inquiry about Cleveland's need for teaching sisters for German parishes. Reverend Westerholt referred the request to Bishop Gilmour.

The sisters initially lived in this house on Huntington Street, provided by the parish. Sister Maria Aloysia taught classes, cooked, and served as superior. The sisters taught at St. Peter School and at St. Stephen, about three miles away on the west side of the Cuyahoga River. (DC.)

In 1873, Cleveland's Bishop Richard Gilmour (1829–1891) requested English-speaking Sisters of Notre Dame for the parish schools of his diocese, prompting the Coesfeld community to bring an Englishwoman to the motherhouse to teach the sisters. In March 1879, Bishop Gilmour presided at Notre Dame's first profession of vows in Cleveland. Among the newly professed was Catherine Franzioni (Sister Mary Anna), the first American to join the congregation.

In fall 1874, the sisters began teaching at Mother of God Parish in Covington, living in this house on Montgomery Street. When Sr. Maria Modesta Többe arrived from Coesfeld in May 1875, she purchased property to build the four-story brick school and convent on Fifth Street, with its chapel dedicated to Mary, the Immaculate Conception. Notre Dame Academy opened in September 1875. From 1875 to 1878, Covington was the congregational motherhouse. (CO.)

The new two-story, six-classroom brick St. Peter School opened in September 1874 with the Brothers of Mary from Dayton teaching the boys, and the Sisters of Notre Dame teaching the girls. Their reputation for excellence brought them to St. Procop (Bohemian) in 1875. By 1880, sisters were teaching in Akron, Delphos, Fremont, Liverpool (now Valley City), Massillon, Norwalk, Rockport (West Park), Toledo, and Burlington, Iowa. St. Peter School closed in 1962. (DC.)

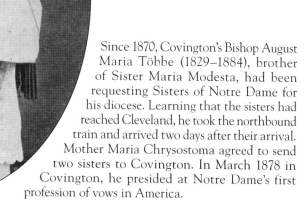

Since 1870, Covington's Bishop August Maria Többe (1829–1884), brother of Sister Maria Modesta, had been requesting Sisters of Notre Dame for his diocese. Learning that the sisters had reached Cleveland, he took the northbound train and arrived two days after their arrival. Mother Maria Chrysostoma agreed to send two sisters to Covington. In March 1878 in Covington, he presided at Notre Dame's first profession of vows in America.

In 1874, the sisters who taught at St. Stephen School on Courtland (now West Fifty-Fourth) Street made the 90-minute trip by horse-drawn tram from the convent at St. Peter until pastor Rev. Casimir Reichlin could build them a residence on Scott (West Fifty-Seventh) Street. Now part of Metro Catholic School, St. Stephen is the longest continuously-held Notre Dame ministry in the United States. (DC.)

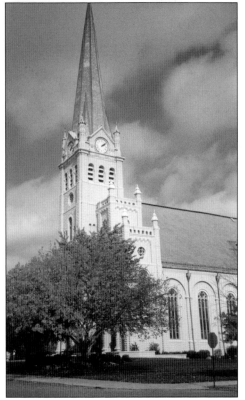

St. John the Evangelist Parish was established in Delphos, Allen County, Ohio, in 1842 by pastor Rev. Otto Bredeick. In 1858, his successor was Rev. Francis Westerholt, who served for 10 years until being called to Cleveland. The Sisters of Notre Dame have staffed the parish school since 1876; in addition, they cared for some elderly parishioners from 1876 to 1906.

Rev. Joseph Koudelka (1852–1921), pastor of newly established St. Michael Church on Scranton Road in Cleveland, welcomed the Sisters of Notre Dame to teach in the parish school in 1882. The elementary school became part of Metro Catholic in 1988; St. Michael High School (1912–1969) became part of Cleveland Central Catholic High School. This second church building, completed in 1892, is listed in the National Register of Historic Places. (CPL.)

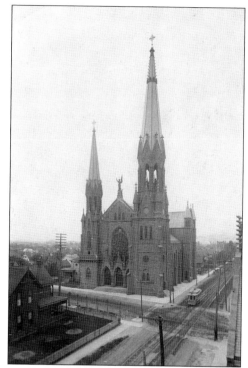

In the summer of 1877, ground was broken at Superior Avenue and Huntington Street for a motherhouse and academy (the small center building). Cleveland's Notre Dame Academy opened to 70 girls in fall 1878. Despite several additions over the next 30 years, including the large 1896 building on the corner (left), the complex became too small for both academy classrooms and the sisters' and novices' living space. (CSU.)

The sisters purchased property at East Ninety-Third Street and Superior Avenue, overlooking Rockefeller Park, in 1912 for this Gothic Revival building, which served as provincial house and novitiate (1915–1960) and as Notre Dame Academy (1915–1963). The Cleveland Board of Education used it as Lulu Diehl Junior High until 1978. Listed in the National Register of Historic Places in 1986, the building was redeveloped by Famicos Foundation as senior apartments in 1999.

Mount St. Mary's Institute opened in 1884 on 11 acres in Woodland Hills (Buckeye Road at Martin Luther King Jr. Boulevard), purchased in 1875 as a potential site for a motherhouse. For 45 years, this protectorate was home and school for hundreds of orphaned girls and those from needy families, and provided a respite for the sisters from the noise and pollution of the industrial city. (DC.)

In the early 1920s, the girls at Mount St. Mary's posed with the sisters and their chaplain, Rev. John Hagan (later the first president of Sisters' College, Cleveland), for a group photograph on the hillside overlooking the city. In this detail from that image, Sr. Mary Pancratia Pohl embraces some of her charges. Sister Mary Pancratia served at Mount St. Mary's from 1918 until it closed in 1929.

Fruits and vegetables from Mount St. Mary's gardens helped feed sisters and students at the convent in the city. The girls played outdoors on the grounds; sisters recuperating from illness benefited from the fresh air. Sister Maria Aloysia spent her last three years at Mount St. Mary's caring for neglected children as she had in Coesfeld in 1849. She died here, age 61, on May 6, 1889.

The sisters relinquished the orphanage ministry in 1929 and sold the property to the Benedictine monks of Cleveland's St. Andrew Abbey, who built Benedictine High School and used this old frame building as their monastery until a new monastery was built. On the south end of the property, on Lamontier Avenue, were the grounds of St. Benedict Church and School. (DC.)

Srs. Mary Verone Wohlwend, Janelle Stracensky, and Luke Arntz paid a final visit to Mount St. Mary's in 1983. The century-old buildings were demolished in 1984 to make way for an addition to St. Andrew Abbey and a new abbey church. In 2014, a memorial stone was laid on the site of the building, commemorating the sisters' ministry on Buckeye Road.

In May 1877, the sisters accepted St. Aloysius Orphanage, Bond Hill, then in a rural area north of Cincinnati, which would house 300 children after the 1918 influenza epidemic. The sisters also served at Cold Spring's St. Joseph and Ft. Mitchell's St. John, and now at Covington's Diocesan Catholic Children's Home, created when the two orphanages merged in 1961. (SND.)

Rev. Joseph Koudelka, former pastor of Cleveland's St. Michael Parish, became bishop of Superior, Wisconsin, in 1913. Four years later, the Sisters of Notre Dame accepted responsibility for St. Joseph Orphan Home in Superior, the fourth orphanage in the sisters' care. This photograph was taken during Mother Maria Caecilia's visit in 1922. The sisters served in Superior until 1943.

From 1898 to 1890, the sisters taught in this school at St. Teresa of Avila, Sheffield, in rural Lorain County, and returned in 1926 when the pastor was able to provide a convent for three sisters. In 1930, Sr. Mary Zitta Meyer was the cook, Sr. Mary George Rhodes taught 45 children in grades 1–4, and Sr. Mary Leonilla Schmuelling taught 27 children in grades 5–8. (DC.)

St. Mary of the Assumption Parish had been serving the people of Elyria for 40 years when the Sisters of Notre Dame arrived in 1899. For a full century, the sisters taught in the parish school and participated in the community. One sister remained in parish ministry at St. Mary until 2006. Opened in 1943, St. Jude Parish had Notre Dame sisters on its school staff from 1950 to 2003. (DC.)

Beginning in 1883, the sisters served at Canton's St. John the Baptist ("the Irish church") until 1919 and at St. Peter ("the German church") until 1997. Because the parishes are just two blocks apart, children of St. Peter's grades 6, 7, and 8 had classes in St. John's building from 1989 to 2002, freeing St. Peter classrooms for kindergarten, preschool, and a library. Sisters directed religious education at St. John from 1999 to 2006. (DC.)

After 1900, high school education became more generally expected. Pastors established parish high schools, generally commercial programs. In addition to the elementary school, St. Francis, Cleveland, offered a two-year commercial course from 1906 to 1940, one of 13 such programs conducted by the sisters. By 1940, commercial programs had been incorporated into comprehensive high school programs at Cleveland's St. Peter, St. Michael, St. Boniface, St. Stephen, and St. Francis. (DC.)

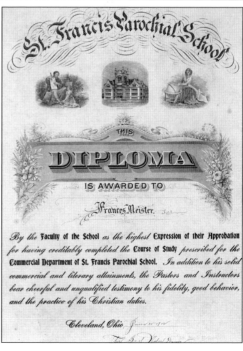

St. Francis Parochial School

THIS

DIPLOMA

IS AWARDED TO

Frances Meister

By the Faculty of the School as the highest Expression of their Approbation for having creditably completed the Course of Study prescribed for the Commercial Department of St. Francis Parochial School. In addition to his solid commercial and literary attainments, the Pastors and Instructors bear cheerful and unqualified testimony to his fidelity, good behavior, and the practice of his Christian duties.

Cleveland, Ohio

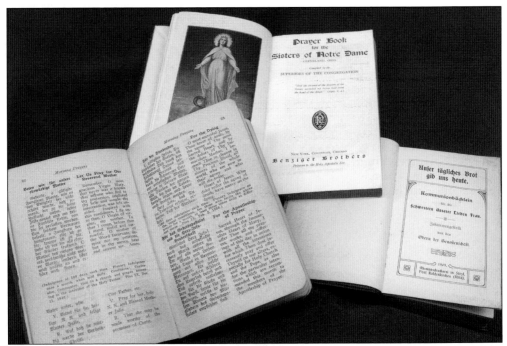

As most Sisters of Notre Dame in the United States were German-born, the language of the community was German until World War I. On the right is the book of communion devotions and prayers used after 1909. In 1917, a German-English community prayer book was published (left), and in 1918 the first annual retreat in English was offered at the Cleveland motherhouse. In 1924, a community prayer book in English came into use (center).

As the Catholic population continued to grow in northwest Ohio, the sisters accepted more schools in cities such as Fostoria, Fremont, Norwalk, Sandusky, and Toledo. In 1877, the sisters began teaching at Toledo's St. Mary Parish, where they staffed the elementary school until 2006. St. Mary was the US community's first commercial high school, operating from 1884 to 1920. (DC.)

When Julie Billiart was declared blessed at St. Peter's, Vatican City, on May 13, 1906, Mother Maria Caecilia Romen, Sr. Mary Louise Kleinmanns, the American provincial superior, and two other sisters were present. In 1909, Mother Maria Caecilia visited Julie's grave at the Namur motherhouse of the Sisters of Notre Dame, beginning an intercommunity friendship that continues to the present.

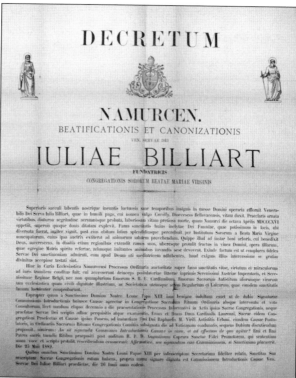

With St. Mary's elementary and high schools thriving in Toledo, the congregation approved the construction of Notre Dame Academy on West Bancroft Street. Opened in 1904, along with art and music schools, the academy building would also be the provincial house after 1924. When 19 counties of northwest Ohio became the Diocese of Toledo in 1910, the sisters were serving in nearly 20 parishes and schools. (TO.)

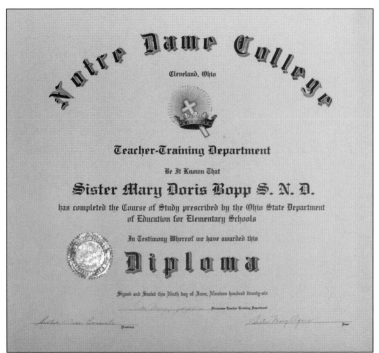

Beginning in 1880, teacher-training classes were part of the postulants' and novices' formation for religious life in a teaching community. As a novice, Sr. Mary Doris Bopp was among the first to earn a two-year elementary teacher training certificate from Notre Dame College in 1926, meeting Ohio's new licensure requirement. With summer and Saturday classes, Sister Mary Doris completed her bachelor's degree in 1940.

As Cleveland's immigrant population from eastern Europe increased, the diocese established more parishes to serve people in their native languages. St. Wendelin was the first Slovak parish served by the Sisters of Notre Dame, who taught in the school from 1903 to 1975. Other Cleveland Slovak parishes staffed by the sisters were St. Ladislas (1905–1928), St. Andrew (1909–1937), Our Lady of Mercy (1921–1935), and SS. Cyril and Methodius, Lakewood (1908–1993). (DC.)

An effective teacher, school administrator, and novice director, Sr. Mary Louise Kleinmanns (1851–1929) became superior of the American province in 1894. During her 24-year ministry, the sisters accepted more than 30 additional schools. Sister Mary Louise supervised the construction of the new provincial house and academy at the Ansel Road property. Under her leadership, the sisters began to use English in the convents as well as in ministry.

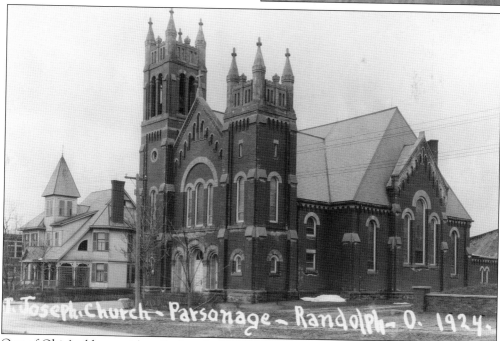

One of Ohio's oldest parishes, St. Joseph, Randolph Township, was established in 1831 to serve German farm families in southern Portage County. The school opened in 1832, St. John Neumann was pastor in 1841, and the Sisters of Notre Dame arrived in 1885 to teach for seven years and again from 1911 to 1918. When a convent was built in 1923, the sisters stayed until 2000.

In 1878, Sr. Mary Gabriele Knappenstein was the first Sister of Notre Dame to die in Cleveland. She was buried at St. Joseph Cemetery on Woodland Avenue at East Seventy-Ninth Street, and is one of 115 Sisters of Notre Dame who rest there. Vandalism in 1992 led to sealing the vault and replacing the grating with a plaque naming the sisters buried there and in a common grave on the hill.

The foundress of the Sisters of Notre Dame, Sr. Maria Aloysia Wolbring, was buried in Cleveland's St. Joseph Cemetery in 1889. In 2008, Srs. Mary Patricia (Vaune) Gannon, Mary (Peter) Brady, Cora Skrivan, Sarah Braun, Elizabeth (Jesslyn) Wood, Madeline (Electa) Columbro, and Brendon Zajac made a pilgrimage to her grave.

Two

GROWTH
1924–1950

Between 1924 and 1950, the Catholic Church in the United States enjoyed vibrant growth. Catholics became part of mainstream American life, and immigrants' children were increasingly Americanized. The Sisters of Notre Dame in Cleveland shared in that growth, welcoming many young women as novices and accepting more schools in a wider geographical range. Ministries outside the classroom expanded as sisters moved into writing textbooks, nursing and other medical specialties, and the foreign missions.

The Cleveland Province sent sisters to Southern California in 1924, opening a mission field that would by 1947 grow to be its own administrative district. In the 1930s and 1940s, the first sisters were assigned to the Washington, DC/Northern Virginia area. As new parishes in the Cleveland diocese opened schools, the sisters accepted 26 new parish schools between 1924 and 1950. After only 35 years, the "new" convent and academy on Ansel Road were at capacity by 1950. Despite the pressures of the Great Depression, Notre Dame College's enrollment nearly doubled between 1930 and 1950.

The province made some bold moves in the years immediately after World War II, venturing briefly into hospital ministry in Tennessee in 1945 and sending missionaries to India in 1949. Having learned from the wartime sufferings endured by the sisters in Europe, the Cleveland community purchased property in Geauga County for a new provincial house away from the industrial city.

Still, excellence in education made the reputation of the Cleveland Sisters of Notre Dame, in kindergartens and elementary schools, in high schools and colleges, in teacher education at Notre Dame and St. John Colleges and Catholic University, and in *Faith and Freedom* readers and *Our Quest for Happiness* religion books. The attractive goodness of the sisters and the grace of God brought growth to the congregation.

With more than 600 sisters in the United States, the congregation restructured the administration of the North American community in 1924 by establishing three separate provinces, in Cleveland, Toledo, and Covington, each with its own provincial house and novitiate. The Covington convent on Fifth Street is shown here. Also in 1924, the sisters accepted two parish schools in the Los Angeles area, laying the foundation for the California Province. (CO.)

At the invitation of pastor Rev. Patrick Pierse, Mother Maria Caecilia sent sisters to St. Matthias in Huntington Park, a growing middle-class town south of Los Angeles. This St. Matthias convent would be the pioneer sisters' gathering place for the next quarter century. Los Angeles became a separate administrative district of the congregation in 1947, with more than 60 sisters serving in seven schools and parishes. (CA.)

In addition to teaching, Sisters of Notre Dame provided domestic services. From 1921 to 1967, sisters cooked at Holy Cross Minor Seminary in South Bend, Indiana. From left to right, Srs. Mary Veronic Roling, Angelene Meyer, and Bernadette Sabovik pose near the Golden Dome. Sisters managed housekeeping at St. Mary Seminary, Cleveland, in the 1920s, and in the 1940s at the University of Portland, Oregon, and at Cleveland's Diocesan Retreat House.

Rev. Joseph Fenelon welcomed the Sisters of Notre Dame to teach at the new parish school of St. Lawrence of Brindisi in Watts in 1924. The town had developed before World War I along a new streetcar line south of Los Angeles, where an ethnically diverse community settled. The five pioneer sisters at St. Lawrence rejoiced in bringing education and catechesis to the very poor. (CA.)

Notre Dame College opened in the former Music House at Ansel Road in September 1922 with 23 students and a faculty made up of four Sisters of Notre Dame, two laywomen, and two priests. Here, Bishop Joseph Schrembs poses with most of the freshmen, with Rockefeller Park behind them. In 1925, a wood-frame building was added to accommodate the growing enrollment. (NDC.)

On 56 acres of farmland on Green Road in South Euclid, Notre Dame College's Tudor Gothic administration building opened for the 1928–1929 academic year, with classrooms, offices, gymnasium, library, kitchen, dining hall, residence hall, and chapel all under one roof. In 1931, when enrollment and staffing reached acceptable levels, the college earned North Central Association accreditation, which has been maintained through 2028. (NDC.)

As dean, Sr. Mary Agnes Bosche encouraged Notre Dame College students to engage in an active intellectual, religious, and social life on campus. Student-organized clubs, lectures, performances, and the Sodality of Our Lady fostered independence and leadership in young women preparing for careers. Here, an advanced seminar discusses philosophy and politics in 1948. Despite the disapproval of Bishop Schrembs, student activities continued to enrich college life. (NDC.)

With construction of the college underway on Green Road, the Sisters of Notre Dame accepted two nearby parish schools, St. Gregory the Great (1925) and Gesu (1926). Sisters teaching at these schools lived at Ansel Road, Marian Hall, or the Catholic Young Women's Hall, traveling on the community bus until convents were built at Gesu in 1948 and at St. Gregory in 1955.

Incorporated in 1908, Idlewood Village had a population of 131 in 1920. Gesu, a Jesuit parish established in 1926, brought the Sisters of Notre Dame to teach in the four-room wooden school building, where these students stand in 1930. With John Carroll University planning to move from West Thirtieth Street, Idlewood was renamed University Heights and grew to 2,237 people by 1930. (GP.)

To serve the Slovak Catholics who settled in Lakewood's Birdtown neighborhood, in 1908 the sisters accepted the school at SS. Cyril and Methodius Parish, where they served until 2000. These 1922 eighth-grade graduates pose with their diplomas outside the school's main entrance on Alameda Avenue. From this class taught by Sr. Mary Norbertine Hilkert, five girls joined the congregation.

At St. Mary, Massillon, Sisters of Notre Dame have taught in the elementary school since 1878, as well as in the parish's commercial high school from 1927 to 1932. These 1949 kindergarteners are learning about houses, sewing drapes, and applying siding. The sisters have been a vibrant presence in Massillon, with 17 young women joining the congregation between 1931 and 1979.

These kindergartners in Sr. Mary Floranne Yatsko's morning class at St. Benedict School, Cleveland, are ready for Halloween in 1946. In the 1940s, when many parish schools added kindergartens, Sr. Mary Marguerite McArdle developed an early childhood curriculum emphasizing "sound physical, mental, spiritual and social training" according to Catholic social principles, including reading readiness, numbers, science, art, and social studies.

Sr. Mary Agatha Markling (right) taught painting to private students, mostly adult women, at the Art House for almost 50 years beginning in 1910. The Art House's 1925 bazaar sales netted nearly $12,000 toward a frame classroom building for the new Notre Dame College on Ansel Road. In 1940, Sr. Mary St. Margaret Mills (left) began assisting with classes and doing commissioned artwork, including calligraphy.

The private classes at the Art House ended when Sister Mary Agatha retired and the provincial center moved to Chardon in 1963, but Sister Mary St. Margaret (left) continued her ministry of fine calligraphy in Marian Studio at Notre Dame College from 1961 to 1973, assisted by Sr. Joanne Marie (St. Kenneth) Zeitz, who continued the work until 1986.

This elegant, hand-carved wooden Nativity set from Germany was a gift to the sisters from Monsignor John Schaffeld, pastor of St. Michael Parish on Scranton Road, in 1929. Many of the figures, repaired and repainted, still adorn the provincial house chapel where Humphrey the camel is a favorite of children who visit at Christmastime.

Sr. Mary Magna Zimmer sits with Notre Dame Academy senior aspirants who became postulants in February 1927, received high school diplomas in June, and became novices in August. During the 1920s, Notre Dame Academy had about 60 aspirants in grades 9–12 each year. Until 1972, the aspirant school nurtured the vocations of high school girls who lived in the convent building during the school year and returned home during vacations.

Rev. Dr. George Johnson, education professor at the Catholic University of America in Washington, DC, established the Campus School in 1936 to put into practice the "whole child" philosophy of education of the Commission on American Citizenship, integrating Christian social principles with rigorous education for life in a democracy.

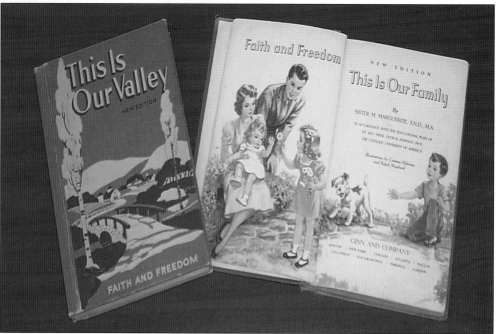

The *Faith and Freedom* readers, originally published by Ginn and Company in the 1940s, were written at the Curriculum Center at Catholic University "to provide children with the basic reading ability to make a living, and with the principles of Christian teaching to make a life," according to Sr. Mary Marguerite McArdle, author of the primary readers. Sister Marguerite was also supervising editor of *Mine* magazine from 1942 to 1963.

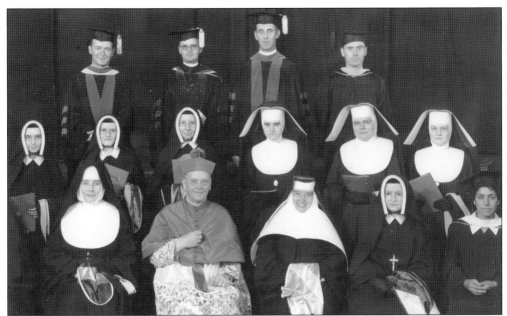

In 1928, the diocese consolidated elementary teacher preparation at Sisters' College (later St. John College) where clergy and religious taught young members of Cleveland's 28 women's congregations. Here, Bishop Joseph Schrembs sits with faculty members, including Sr. Mary Vera Niess. Notre Dame sisters taught at St. John until 1946. Graduating in 1934 were Srs. Mary Eugenius Zimmerman, Juanita Vintar, and Adalrike Stockhorst (second row).

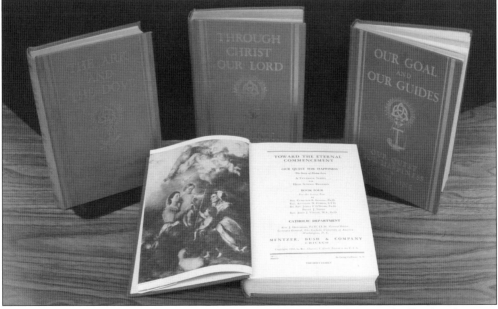

As superintendent of Cleveland's Catholic schools, Monsignor Dr. Clarence Elwell enlisted a group of experienced teachers (religious and priests) to write and illustrate a set of religion textbooks for high schools. Srs. Mary St. Therese Dunn, Agera Gerke, and Florice Keaveny studied, planned, wrote, and illustrated the series from 1940 to 1948. The *Our Quest for Happiness* series was used in hundreds of dioceses through the 1960s and remains in print.

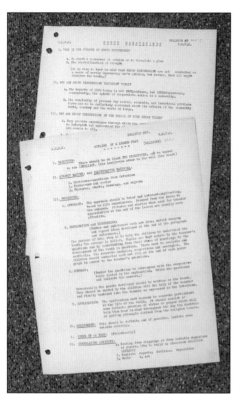

After the death of Sr. Mary Girolama Lehmkuhl in 1922, Sr. Mary Fortunata Horning (1871–1954) was supervisor of community elementary schools, which involved traveling with the provincial superior to visit every sister's classroom and coaching and encouraging teachers, children, and principals. Her *School Bulletin* included both practical and spiritual advice for religious teachers. In 1945, Sr. Mary Floracita Renner became her assistant; Sr. Mary Alicia Miday was the first high school supervisor.

Established in 1936, St. Agnes Parish, Arlington, Virginia, built a school and convent 10 years later and welcomed five Sisters of Notre Dame as faculty. The sisters taught at St. Agnes through 2009. Sisters later served in other area parishes, including St. Ann, Arlington; St. Leo, Fairfax; All Saints, Manassas; St. John, McLean; St. John, Warrenton; Sacred Heart, Winchester; and Our Lady of Victory, Washington, DC.

In 1945, the Sisters of Notre Dame accepted St. Mary Hospital in Humboldt, Tennessee. Several sisters were educated as medical professionals, including Sr. Mary Amedia Beckman, a medical technologist. St. Mary thrived during the sisters' ministry, which ended suddenly in 1954 because of the great need for schoolteachers. However, a number of sister-nurses from St. Mary later used their medical training in the India mission.

After 20 years of teaching, Sr. Mary Clare O'Neill (1891–1964) used her master's in religion and philosophy from the University of Notre Dame in a ministry of social activism, including a weekly diocesan newspaper column, the *Family Front*, research on comic books' cultural values, and the Mary/Patrick/Martin de Porres Workshop providing counseling, study groups, and legal and financial aid. The woman on her left became Sr. Mary Roseclare Kulbaga.

After the 1915 move to the new building at Ansel Road and Superior Avenue, the old provincial center building at East Seventeenth Street and Superior Avenue was converted to the Catholic Young Women's Hall, providing housing for professional women, students, visitors to Cleveland, religious sisters studying in Cleveland, and Sisters of Notre Dame serving in parishes without convents. (CSU.)

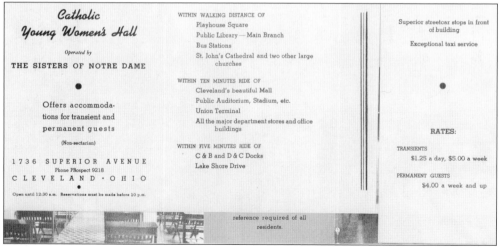

For more than 25 years, the Catholic Young Women's Hall was home to both permanent and transient residents. In 1949, the year of peak occupancy, there were 156 residents and staff. As many as 15 sisters and 18 laypeople provided the residents with food service and housekeeping, as well as days of recollection, retreats, and study groups. In 1956, the sisters sold the property to the Diocese of Cleveland.

The first American-born major superior, Sr. Mary Evarista Harks (1867–1943), was a child at St. Peter School when the Sisters of Notre Dame arrived in 1874. In her 25-year ministry as Cleveland's first provincial superior, she guided the community through a period of major expansion and growth despite the difficulties of the Great Depression and World War II.

In 1971, St. Peter High School, Lourdes Academy, and St. Stephen High School merged to form Erieview Catholic High School for girls, staffed by the Sisters of the Humility of Mary and lay teachers. When Erieview closed in 1993, the building became the Bishop William M. Cosgrove Center, a major center for the Diocese of Cleveland's social outreach ministry.

On October 20, 1944, two of four tanks of liquefied natural gas exploded at the East Ohio Gas facility just north of St. Clair Avenue at East Sixty-First Street. During the two-day fire, more than 130 people died, 81 buildings were destroyed, and 20 city blocks burned. Sisters teaching at St. Vitus School, two blocks from the explosion, evacuated the children by walking them south, away from St. Clair.

Novices and postulants enjoy a springtime recreation at Ansel Road in 1945. Like many other religious congregations, Notre Dame welcomed many vocations in the years after World War II. In summer 1945, thirteen postulants joined fifty-seven novices in the novitiate community, and fifteen novices professed first vows. In the background, the dome of St. Thomas Aquinas Church is visible across Superior Avenue.

This spacious redbrick Colonial building on four acres on Overland Avenue in West Los Angeles was purchased in 1945 to provide a center for sisters in the eight California houses. In April 1946, classes began at Notre Dame Elementary School. At Easter 1947, it became the home of Rosa Mystica District, with Sr. Mary Loyole Gabel as district superior. The first postulants began their formation in California in 1948. (CA.)

In Cleveland's Calvary Cemetery, established in 1893, one hundred seventy-six Sisters of Notre Dame are buried. In 1920, Sr. Mary Josepha Pahl was the first to be laid to rest in Section 41. At the base of this monument are memorials to provincial superiors Mother Mary Louise Kleinmanns (d. 1929 in Germany), Mother Mary Evarista Harks (d. 1943), and foundress Sr. Maria Aloysia Wolbring, buried at St. Joseph Cemetery in 1889.

During World War II, US Sisters of Notre Dame supported American efforts through prayer, action, and commitment to patriotism with the students and in the community, while trying to maintain contact with family and sisters in Germany. Notre Dame College students Phoebe Burbridge, Genet Broadbent, Marian Kresl, and Jeanne Kirby sold war bonds on campus. After 1945, the sisters sent many care packages to sisters and relatives in Germany. (NDC.)

In the 1944–1945 school year, Cleveland's St. Michael High School had its first twelfth-graders, but only 43 of the 200 students that year were boys. At the May 27, 1945, graduation, 35 girls and four boys received diplomas, two of the boys in absentia, already serving in the military. One attended in his US Navy uniform, having been granted furlough to attend the ceremony.

Shamrock Acres was a 140-acre dairy farm in Munson Township in Geauga County, about 20 miles east of Cleveland. In 1948, the sisters purchased the farm with its 15 cows, dairy facilities, pasture, sugarhouse, and woodlands. They intended to build a new provincial house there. Conferring with John Diersen near the farmhouse in 1948 are, from left to right, provincial superior Mother Mary Agnes and Srs. Mary Jeanita Fitz and Bertilda Hillinhinrichs.

John Diersen and son Alan meet Josi the calf at Shamrock Acres. Since calves were named for the saints on whose feast day they were born, Josi probably arrived on March 19, 1949, St. Joseph's day. John Diersen's uncle Henry Diersen came from Germany in 1882 and worked for the sisters on Superior Avenue, at Ansel Road, and at Mount St. Mary's until his death in 1938.

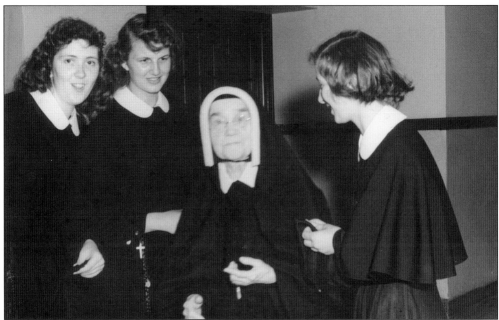

A grand celebration of the 75th anniversary of the arrival of the Sisters of Notre Dame in the United States was held on July 4, 1949, at Notre Dame College, with sisters from Toledo and Covington traveling to Cleveland for the day. Here, one of the oldest sisters of the Cleveland Province, Sr. Mary Berchmans Seifert, meets with the youngest members (from left to right), postulants Rita Brady, Patricia Pasek, and Dorothy Turk.

After celebrating morning Mass at the various summer residences in northern Ohio, sisters gathered at Notre Dame College for the 75th anniversary festivities. Here, a busload of sisters from Toledo receives a hearty welcome at the college on a hot, sunny July 4, 1949. A good time was had by all. There were more than 1,100 sisters in the United States in 1949.

At St. John Cathedral on August 28, 1949, six Sisters of Notre Dame were officially missioned to Patna, India, the first overseas missionaries from the Cleveland diocese. Bishop Edward F. Hoban presented the mission cross to Sr. Mary Magdela Shaeffer. Other pioneers were Srs. Mary St. Thomas Fitzgerald, Maris Geiger, Joelle Luebbers, Kieran Seubert, and Lauretta Thompson. Over the next 16 years, 12 more sisters were missioned to Patna. (DC.)

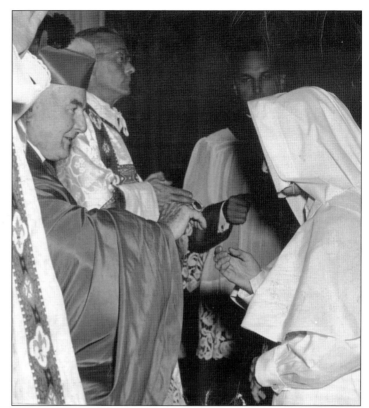

Bishop Augustine Wildermuth welcomed the sisters on their arrival in Patna on October 30, 1949. Within a year, the sisters had opened a clinic and were teaching in schools in both English and Hindi. In 1953, Notre Dame Academy opened in Jamalpur, and in 1956, the first Indian postulants were welcomed. In 2019, the two provinces, Patna and Bangalore, have nearly 300 professed sisters and 25 novices.

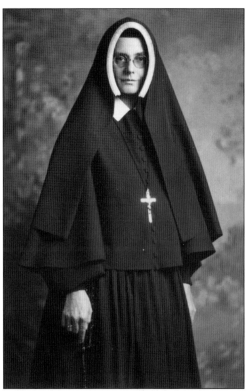

Sr. Mary Agnes Bosche (1885–1949) was charged with establishing Notre Dame College in 1922, creating the curriculum, hiring faculty, locating physical and financial resources, and guiding student life. After 12 years as dean, she later served as principal at Notre Dame Academy before assuming community leadership. She was Cleveland's much-loved provincial superior for less than two years before her death at age 64.

Elected superior general in 1946, Mother Mary Vera Niess fulfilled the congregation's decades-long dream of locating the international motherhouse near the Vatican. This villa in Rome's Monte Mario district on Via della Camilluccia was purchased in 1948, expanded, and ready for the general administration to arrive in 1949. In the large chapel, sisters prayed day and night before the Blessed Sacrament for the congregation and the world.

Three

EXPANSION
1950–1975

The middle of the 20th century marked a high point in the Cleveland Province in terms of membership and ministries; it was a time of wide-ranging adaptation through alertness to the signs of the times.

As the baby boom generation started kindergarten in the early 1950s, Catholic schools coped with unprecedented enrollment. Between 1950 and 1975, the sisters accepted 52 new schools, half of them in Ohio, with others in Florida, Northern Virginia/District of Columbia, and North Carolina. Sisters were teaching in 13 high schools, four owned by the sisters. Increased enrollment required building projects to expand elementary schools, high schools, and Notre Dame College.

Growth in the India mission led to Patna's becoming Assumption Province in 1958, and the Southern California district became Rosa Mystica Province in 1961. The growth in Cleveland—there were 77 novices in 1957—made it clear that the Ansel Road building was no longer adequate, leading to a new provincial house, novitiate, infirmary, and academy in Geauga County between 1958 and 1964.

Vatican Council II's call for the renewal of religious life began a time marked by hope and tension. The congregation and the Chardon Province approached renewal slowly and cautiously, frustrating sisters who had hoped for more immediate change in community living and in ministries. Nearly 200 sisters requested dispensation from their vows or transferred to other religious congregations in the Cleveland area or headed to Pueblo, Colorado, to experiment with a new form of dedicated life.

A special general chapter in 1968 and Julie Billiart's canonization in 1969 revitalized the spirit of Notre Dame. Understanding consecrated life as rooted in the Scriptures, church documents, and the writings of St. Julie, the sisters began to reenvision their lives not as monastic but as apostolic women religious, attentive to and engaged with the world, rooted in deep prayer, living what St. Julie called "rapture of action."

After a distinguished career as classroom teacher and professor of education at Cleveland's St. John College, Sr. Mary Vera Niess (1902–1962) became provincial superior in July 1943, but served less than four years before becoming superior general in 1946 after the death of Mother Maria Antonie Sommer. Sr. Mary Vera Niess's energy, scholarship, and spirituality led the congregation to a new motherhouse in Rome and into its second century.

During the centennial, Sr. Mary Germaine Hoeffel designed the congregation's coat of arms. The Cross of Jesus is central, surmounted by the dove representing the Holy Spirit. The lily and star of the sea represent Mary. The eagle is adapted from the arms of Germany, the congregation's origin; the lion rampant echoes the arms of Belgium (Namur) and the Netherlands (Amersfoort); the fleur-de-lis roundels represent France, Julie Billiart's birthplace.

During the 1950 centennial, the congregation held an educational institute at the new generalate in Rome, addressing the principles, traditions, and experiences of Notre Dame educators around the world as part of a program of spiritual renewal. Participants had the privilege of a private audience with Pope Pius XII, with Mother Mary Vera Niess on the Holy Father's right.

A loan from the Cleveland diocese, Marian Hall on East Boulevard, east of Liberty Boulevard, was a stately three-story mansion that could house 40 sisters. Marian Hall was first a residence for teachers in schools that did not have convents. For nearly 10 years, it was the community infirmary. When the Chardon infirmary was completed in 1960, the community returned the building to the diocese.

Campus School eighth-graders make their civics presentation in the late 1950s when Srs. Mary Robert Taylor and St. Jude Weisensell taught junior high. Staffed by the Sisters of Notre Dame from 1936 until 1969, Campus School was a demonstration school and site for Catholic University student teachers. Srs. Mary Verone Wohlwend, Vernice Makovic, and DeXavier Perusek were professors in Catholic University's education department during those years.

Seventh-graders in Sr. Mary Virginette Ackerman's class at St. Gregory the Great, South Euclid, demonstrate their mastery of sentence structure in 1959. Enrollment at St. Gregory School peaked in 1968 at 955 students in grades 1–8.

The Julie Billiart School for children with special learning needs relocated to the Arter mansion in Lyndhurst in 1958, four years after opening at Ansel Road. Sr. Mary Marguerite McArdle (1904–1993), formerly diocesan education supervisor and director of student teachers at St. John College and Catholic University, did graduate study in special education as preparation for guiding Julie Billiart School through its first eight years. (JB.)

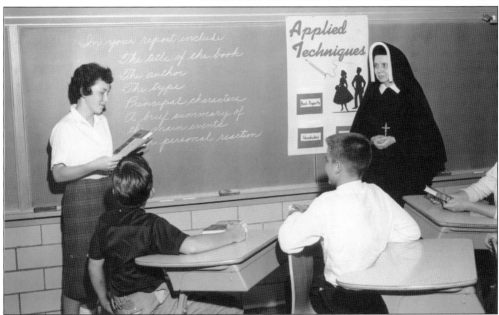

Sr. Mary Marcella Zimmerman helps her seventh-graders prepare a public speaking assignment at St. Francis of Assisi School in Gates Mills. The parish was established in 1943 to serve Catholics who lived along the Mayfield Road corridor between South Euclid's St. Gregory the Great and Chardon's St. Mary Parishes. The sisters staffed the school from its opening in 1954 until 1999.

Students, faculty, and guests gather for Regina High School's 1954 dedication. Construction had begun in October 1951 on Green Road, west of Notre Dame College. When classes began in September 1953, eight sister-teachers and a staff of 14 welcomed 116 freshmen and 36 sophomores. By 1958, more than 550 students were pursuing a college-preparatory curriculum, filling the 25 classrooms. The need for expansion was clear.

A 1961 addition gave Regina High School 20 more classrooms and a convent for more than 40 sisters; in 1971, a 1,000-seat auditorium was added. Regina's enrollment peaked at 1,170 in 1968, with students from urban, suburban, and rural areas in Cuyahoga, Lake, and Geauga Counties. It was a richly diverse group of young women gifted in academics, arts, and athletics. Sr. Sally (Ruthanne) Huston coached the 1979 tennis team.

Established by the Diocese of Cleveland in 1948, Elyria Catholic High School moved into its own building the following year and awarded its first diplomas to 17 graduates in 1950. The Sisters of Notre Dame served at Elyria Catholic from its beginnings until 2003. Here, Rev. Dr. Joseph Lehane, director, and Rev. Lawrence Budny, pastor of Elyria's Holy Cross Parish, inspect the construction site on Gulf Road in 1948.

Sr. Mary Noreen Hansel's 1966 students prepare liturgy at St. Mary, Warren, where the sisters staffed the elementary school (1922–1971) and high school (1944–1964). The Youngstown diocese dedicated John F. Kennedy High School in 1964 and in 1971 created a consolidated St. Mary Middle School (later Notre Dame School), where the sisters continued until 2003. Today, JFK includes both lower campus (pre-K–5) and upper school (grades 6–12).

Throughout the 1950s, the farm at Shamrock Acres offered the sisters picnic days during vacations. In the summer of 1955, from left to right, Srs. Mary Coramarie Santill, St. Dominic Nudo, Reean Coyne, and Kathleen Scully enjoy an afternoon of games on Auburn Road.

The sisters purchased Ivanhoe Farm, across Auburn Road from Shamrock Acres, in 1957. With 175 acres of pasture, orchards, and woods, a herd of beef cattle, and two homes with outbuildings, this land became the site of the new provincial center. From left to right, postulants Molly O'Connor, Barbara Knuff, and Joan Klasson enjoy a break from their college studies by picking pears in 1961.

Provincial superior Mother Mary Anselm Langenderfer (right, 1905–1991) and Sr. Mary Elise Krantz depart in 1951 for a first visit to the Patna, India, mission. Sister Mary Anselm had been Cleveland's novice director before becoming provincial (1949–1961) and then California's first provincial in 1961. Kind and soft-spoken, Mother Anselm served as superior general from 1962 to 1974 and then returned to Chardon for her last years.

The sisters purchased property in Hidden Valley, northwest of Los Angeles, in 1957 for a novitiate. Rancho La Pilarica offered solitude for California's postulants and novices during their spiritual formation and their early college studies. The provincial center moved from Overland Avenue to La Pilarica in 1965. A new provincial center and novitiate in nearby Thousand Oaks was completed in 1979.

By 1958, the Cleveland Province, with more than 700 sisters, stretched from Virginia to California. To ease the workload of the provincial superior, the new Julie Billiart Province, led by Mother Mary Joseph Geise, was created in Canton, Ohio, on a 49-acre estate. The province's main educational ministry was a kindergarten begun by Sr. Jeanne Mary (Jane Frances) Nieminen in the Everhard Road mansion.

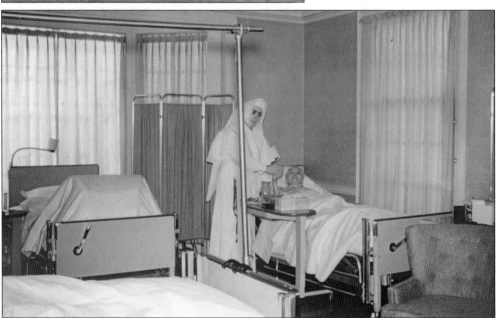

At the Maryhill Convalescent Home, Sr. Mary Roman Ress tends to a patient in a ward created in the living room of the mansion. Located on a 17-acre estate adjoining the larger Everhard Road property, Maryhill served 82 patients in its nine-year existence. Its lovely formal gardens provided a restful atmosphere for recuperation.

Mother Mary Joseph Geise (1894–1987), former Covington provincial superior, led the Julie Billiart Province from 1959 to 1963. Plans for a provincial house, novitiate, and girls' high school at the Everhard Road property never materialized, but the sisters remember Mother Mary Joseph's warm and holy leadership. When the Canton and Cleveland Provinces were reunited in 1963, Sister Mary Joseph returned to Covington, and the Canton property was sold in 1967. (SND.)

Notre Dame Elementary School's first first-graders wait patiently for their teacher, Sr. Mary Daniel Buescher, in their Shamrock Acres classroom in 1958. Ten years later, Notre Dame Elementary had moved into the west end of the teacher training wing. By 1963, Sisters of Notre Dame staffed all Catholic elementary schools in Geauga County: St. Mary, Chardon (established 1961), St. Helen, Newbury (1961), and St. Anselm, Chesterland (1963), as well as Notre Dame.

In summer 1962, construction of Regina Mundi Chapel was underway on the east end (right) of the new Chardon provincial center. The new teacher training wing on the west (white-roofed) was home to 68 novices, 33 postulants, 42 aspirants, and many sisters under temporary vows. On the south end (below), Resurrection Cemetery was being prepared. Sr. Mary Ethelreda Strohmeyer was the first burial in May 1963.

With the first wings of the new Chardon building complete in fall 1959, the provincial administration made the move from Ansel Road. The infirmary patients moved in February 1960, and in May, construction began on the teacher training wing, west of the administration wing. Two years later, in May 1962, these sisters gathered at the administration wing's main entrance to break ground for Regina Mundi Chapel.

With daily liturgy and exposition of the Blessed Sacrament, Regina Mundi Chapel has been the center of life at the provincial center. The life-sized crucifix surmounted by a crown-shaped *baldachino* illustrate the Paschal Mystery: Christ as King. With its glistening terrazzo floor, and its marble altar, lectern, and communion stations, the semicircular sanctuary reflected the liturgical renewal of Vatican II, emphasizing the full and active participation of the community.

Understanding and singing liturgical music was an important part of the young sisters' formation. Led by Sister Mary Madonne (Mary Lou Skirbunt), a choir of 150 postulants, novices, and professed sisters produced a recording of 18 Advent/Christmas songs, *A Child Is Born*, in autumn 1965. The 3,000 albums sold immediately. This choir of young sisters performed a series of Easter concerts in Chardon in April 1968.

Notre Dame Academy opened in Geauga County in September 1963 with 282 students, including 22 boarders, holding classes in the houses and barns of the Raible farm on Butternut Road, adjacent to the former Ivanhoe Farm. This new brick academy building, opposite the barns, was ready for use in January 1965. Enrollment at Chardon Notre Dame Academy reached an all-time-high of 955 in the 1969–1970 school year. (CSU.)

From 1963 until the boarding school closed in 1979, sisters served as dorm moderators, food service staff, and supportive presence, living in the residences with the girls. This group of sisters and students enjoys dinner before a school dance in November 1968. Residence hall staff included Srs. Marla Loehr, Mary Joeleen Knorr, Jacquelyn (Evarista) Gusdane, Renetta Graff, and Mary Ann (Brigid) Burke.

In their first year at the Chardon campus, Georgina Kindall, Andrea Zadell, Catherine Matjasic, and Stephanie Alsenas, senior editors of Notre Dame Academy's newspaper the *Tower*, were adjusting to classrooms in farmhouses, converted barns, and temporary buildings. The blue uniforms worn at Ansel Road would be replaced by gray-and-red plaid skirts with gray blazers as the academy developed new traditions based on the school's 85-year-old foundations.

On Notre Dame Day 1969, the class of 1973 emerges from Freshman Hall wearing the new blue-white-and-gold checked uniform skirt with a blue blazer. Two corridors of portable classrooms between the assembly hall and the boarding school were ninth-grade homerooms until the 1979 addition gave the academy a new library, additional classrooms, and faculty office space.

The Notre Dame Guild was made up of the sisters' relatives and friends and alumnae of the academy and the college who supported the ministries of the sisters through card parties, luncheons, lectures, and days of recollection. Rev. Patrick Peyton, the "Rosary Priest" who founded Holy Cross Family Ministries, was a scheduled speaker in December 1945.

The fundraising activities of the Notre Dame Guild included raffles with impressive prizes like cash or automobiles for the winners, as well as sellers' prizes. Academy students worked alongside the sisters when events were held at the Ansel Road convent. Sr. Mary Bernita Holtgrieve, longtime moderator of the guild, also sold handmade robes for Infant of Prague statues.

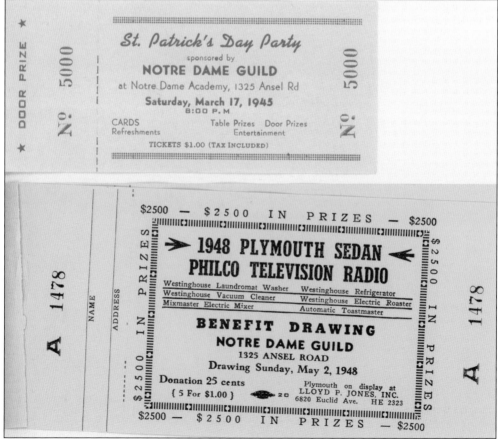

St. Patrick's Day Party
sponsored by
NOTRE DAME GUILD
at Notre Dame Academy, 1325 Ansel Rd
Saturday, March 17, 1945
8:00 P.M

DOOR PRIZE ★   N°. 5000   5000 N°.

CARDS   Table Prizes Door Prizes
Refreshments   Entertainment
        TICKETS $1.00 (TAX INCLUDED)

★

$2500 — $2500 IN PRIZES — $2500

→ 1948 PLYMOUTH SEDAN ←
PHILCO TELEVISION RADIO
Westinghouse Laundromat Washer   Westinghouse Refrigerator
Westinghouse Vacuum Cleaner   Westinghouse Electric Roaster
Mixmaster Electric Mixer   Automatic Toastmaster

BENEFIT DRAWING
NOTRE DAME GUILD
1325 ANSEL ROAD
Drawing Sunday, May 2, 1948

Donation 25 cents   Plymouth on display at
{ 5 For $1.00 }   ←2○ LLOYD P. JONES, INC.
                               6820 Euclid Ave.   HE 2323

$2500 — $2500 IN PRIZES — $2500

A 1478 $2500 IN PRIZES $2500 IN PRIZES   A 1478

NAME ADDRESS

Having assisted Sister Mary Fortunata for three years, Sr. Mary Elreda Buescher (1908–2005) became community supervisor in 1952. Here, Sister Elreda and high school supervisor Sr. Mary Owen Kleinhenz (center) made a visit in 1979 to Notre Dame Montessori School, Chardon, with (from left to right) Srs. Maria Constansa Baggan, Juvina Esseling, and Maria Lutharde Icks from Germany.

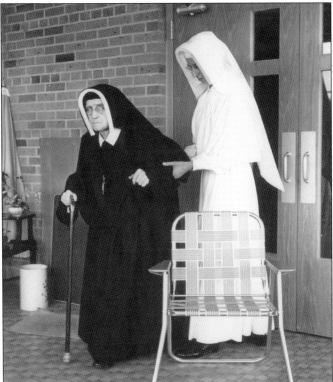

Sr. Mary Anne (Emeric) Blasko guides Sr. Mary Laura Helten to her chair in the solarium at the south end of the new infirmary. When the Chardon infirmary opened in February 1960, nine sisters were bed patients. After the 1974 O'Neill Wing was added, the infirmary's capacity was 47. By 1994, 43 sisters were receiving full nursing care, with 25 more receiving some assistance.

In the hunt country near Middleburg, Loudoun County, Virginia, the Hitt estate became Notre Dame Academy in September 1965, with two Sisters of Notre Dame teaching seven ninth-graders (five boarders and two day students) and Sr. Mary Frances (Donald Ann) Dunham serving as principal. The following year, enrollment was 20 students. Steady growth led to a 1968 ground breaking for a classroom/dormitory building. The first senior class graduated in 1969.

In May 1969, Bishop John Russell of Richmond was the main celebrant of the dedication of Notre Dame Academy's new building in Middleburg. Classrooms, offices, laboratories for science and art, and a music room were connected to the mansion by this breezeway. The upper floor provided dorm rooms for 40 residents and two faculty. In fall 1969, Notre Dame Academy enrolled 135 girls in grades 8–12, including 76 residents.

Notre Dame's presence in Northern Virginia grew after the academy opened in Middleburg. At Sacred Heart, Winchester, Sr. Mary Doreen Strahler and her students observe construction of the new church. By 1973, the sisters were also teaching at St. John in Warrenton, St. Leo in Fairfax, and St. John in McLean. Growth in the region led to the 1974 creation of the Arlington diocese, serving Virginia's 21 northern counties.

The Sisters of Notre Dame arrived at Our Lady of Lourdes, Dunedin, and St. Mary Magdalen, Maitland, in 1965, and accepted ministry at Clearwater Central Catholic in 1971. Here, Rev. William DuBois joins Srs. Mary de Angelis Bothwell, Josellen Dajer, Jeanne Mary Nieminen, Richard Anne Ullman, and Therese (Eduard) White. Over the years, the sisters maintained a strong presence in Florida's Orlando, St. Petersburg, and Venice dioceses.

After a 1964 liturgy at St. Stephen Church celebrating the 90th anniversary of the community's arrival in Cleveland, Sr. Mary Concepta Pavlac greeted friends who shared the celebration. Sister Mary Concepta had taught primary children at St. Stephen for 16 years between 1934 and 1954, and had served as St. Stephen's principal from 1961 to 1963.

These sisters are leaving St. Peter Church on Superior Avenue in 1964 following another 90th anniversary Mass. On the steps are Srs. Mary Theresine Neumann and St. Martha Conrad; among those on the sidewalk are Srs. Mary Muriel Petrasek, Rosemary (St. Ignatius) Mayer, Teresita Gresko, and Leone Blank.

With the teacher training wing completed in 1963, sixty Notre Dame aspirants relocated from Ansel Road to Chardon. With the older students in Regina uniforms and the younger ones in academy skirts and blazers, this group enjoys an afternoon music session. Standing are Bonita Zajac, Alice Koporc, Patricia Sipan, Meribeth Rome, Mary Ann Brewster, and Mary Ann Muzick; seated are Olivia Latiano, Mary Ann Fekete, and Janet Schemmel.

After the changes sparked by Vatican Council II, many religious left their congregations. About 150 Sisters of Notre Dame (two-thirds with perpetual vows) left the community between 1965 and 1970. Nevertheless, the Chardon Province numbered nearly 700 sisters in 1970, when (from left to right) postulants Audrey Wright and Rita Brunst joined Srs. Mary Donnalee Resar, Jane Therese Thein, and postulant Jeannie Alfieri for a Sunday stroll.

Mother Mary Elise Krantz (1913–2007) served as Chardon's provincial superior from 1961 to 1973. During her tenure, the move of the provincial house, infirmary, novitiate, and academy to the Chardon property was completed, and sisters were missioned to many new schools. In the turbulent years after Vatican Council II, Mother Elise strove to maintain a style of religious life faithful to the church's vision.

Endorsing a cautious interpretation of the council's call to renew religious life as outlined in the 1966 decree *Perfectae Caritatis*, some bishops and superiors of congregations established the Consortium Perfectae Caritatis in 1970. After a 1974 liturgy at Rome's Basilica of San Clemente, Mother Marie William MacGregor, OP; Mother Mary Elise Krantz, SND; Mother Mary Bernadette Wiseman, PBVM; and Rev. James Viall converse with Cardinal Egidio Vagnozzi.

Directed by Monsignor Dr. Eugene Kevane (1913–1996), the Notre Dame Institute for Advanced Studies in Religious Education was established in Middleburg in 1969 to prepare sisters to teach Catholic doctrine. Institute summer classes led to an advanced catechetical diploma and a master's in religious education. Arlington's Bishop Thomas Welsh awarded the 1978 diplomas. After moving to Arlington in 1975, the institute became the Notre Dame Graduate School of Virginia's Christendom College.

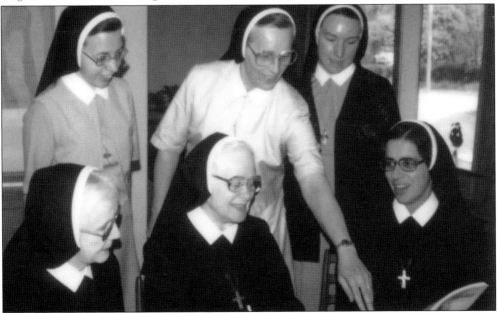

During the 1970s and 1980s, the sisters researched, wrote, and illustrated the *Christ Our Life* religion textbook series for grades 1–8, published by Loyola Press, with lessons tested in 52 Notre Dame schools before publication. Here, the 1984 junior high staff reviews a draft. From left to right are (seated) Srs. Mary David Horan, de Angelis Bothwell, and Patricia Rickard; (standing) Srs. Mary Renée (Stephany) Pastor, Verne Kavula, and Mary Reiling. Classroom and family catechists use the 2016 edition's print and online resources.

Seven Chardon sisters were among hundreds of Sisters of Notre Dame in St. Peter's Basilica on June 22, 1969, for the canonization of Julie Billiart by Pope Paul VI. The Rome motherhouse hosted more than 50 sisters for three days of celebrations. Among the Brazilian pilgrims was Otacilio Ribeiro, whose 1950 cure in the Notre Dame hospital in Campos Novos was the final miracle needed for Julie's canonization.

Since 1959, more than a dozen sisters from India have earned degrees in Cleveland and Cincinnati. In 1972, newly arrived Notre Dame College students, from left to right, Sisters Mary Pratima, Dulari, Priya, and Jayanti gathered with mission procurator Sr. Marie Clarice (Nathaniel) Bates (center front) and Patna provincial Mother Mary St. Thomas Fitzgerald and Sr. Mary Kieran Seubert. This shared ministry built international friendships among Patna, Bangalore, Chardon, and Covington.

In 1969, Sisters of Notre Dame staffed Our Lady of Lourdes and St. Michael High Schools, which merged with St. John Cantius and St. Stanislaus High Schools to form Cleveland Central Catholic, led by Fr. John Fiala. The innovative high school offered expanded opportunities for its 1,600 students. As enrollment declined, operations focused on the Slavic Village campus at St. Stanislaus, where sisters continue as administrators and teachers.

St. Aloysius Parish School in East Liverpool, Ohio, was a ministry of the Sisters of Notre Dame from 1944 through 1998. Before the start of the 1974 school year, a ride on a restored steam locomotive entertained Srs. Theresa May (St. Cecilia) Grohosky, Carol Marie (Carmeleen) Urmetz, Mary Zeno Lemmerman, St. Jane Rohr, Geralyn Stenger, and friends. Legendary football coach Lou Holtz (class of 1951) appreciated his rigorous education at St. Aloysius.

The sisters who staffed the Chardon sewing room provided each sister with two custom-made habits until 1973, when ready-made dresses were purchased and altered individually to each sister's measurements. From left to right, Srs. Mary Joela Leinberger, Linda Marie Conrad, Mary Ann (Orrin) Brewster, Constance (Levan) Przybylski, and Marie (Magdaleen) Soboslay are hard at work in 1975.

In 1968, a generous benefactor provided a swimming pool to enhance the sisters' health and fitness. After 30 years of use, the pool was repaired and upgraded. Here, Srs. Mary Dina Prebaneck, Frances Murray, and Luke Arntz rededicate the waters in 1997, with Srs. Mary Catherine (St. Myles) Caine, Antonee Pfenning, and Francismarie Seiler participating. The space became Notre Dame Elementary's multipurpose room in 2019.

Four

REFOCUSING
1975–2000

After a century in the United States, the Chardon Sisters of Notre Dame continued their excellent teaching and teacher education, focusing energy and resources particularly on schools in the urban centers. With fewer sisters in active ministry, more lay colleagues took on administrative and teaching roles. The sisters worked in increasingly collaborative settings such as Cleveland's Metro Catholic School and the Youngstown diocese's consolidated Catholic schools. Notre Dame Academy, Chardon, connected with the legacy of Cathedral Latin School to launch Notre Dame–Cathedral Latin in 1988. Beginning with Notre Dame College in 1990, the schools owned and operated by the sisters began the shift to a sponsorship model of governance with decision-making boards of trustees composed of laywomen and -men as well as Sisters of Notre Dame.

The ongoing spiritual formation of the sisters became an even greater priority in these years. Living in smaller groups, serving in more individual ministries, sisters became more intentional about personal wholeness and community living. The establishment of Bethany Retreat Center in 1981 made possible a wider variety of retreats for smaller groups of sisters throughout the year. The focus on spiritual growth led more sisters to ministries of parish leadership, spiritual direction, and spiritual care.

Led by Srs. Maria Raphaelita Böckmann (superior general from 1974 to 1986), Mary Joell Overman (1986–1998), and Mary Sujita Kallupurakkuthu (1998–2010), the congregation grew in collaboration and internationality. Through the 1982 National Congress, hundreds of sisters began to cultivate friendships and mutual understanding across provincial boundaries. After the 1983 International Congress on Our Apostolates, held in Chardon, congregational leaders began methodically sharing resources for spirituality and ministry in the United States and around the world. Spirituality and internationality became central to the sisters' lives.

After a brief stint in research with Goodyear in Akron, Sr. Mary Christopher Rohner (1923–1983) taught at Notre Dame College for 20 years, earned a doctorate from Fordham, worked with the residents, and published her research. After becoming provincial superior in 1973, Sister Mary Christopher energetically promoted the sisters' spiritual life, and guided implementation of the new Rule of Life.

At the 1974–1975 General Chapter, delegates charted congregational renewal, elected Sr. Maria Raphaelita Böckmann as superior general, and drafted a new Rule of Life, or constitutions, for the congregation. Before departing for Rome, these Chardon delegates prayed at Sister Maria Aloysia's grave in St. Joseph Cemetery. From left to right are Srs. Mary Owen Kleinhenz, Jane Elizabeth Sakach, Christopher Rohner, Jonathan Zeleznik, Marthe Reinhard, and Margaret (Nathan) Hess.

Sisters stationed at the congregation's motherhouse in Rome often visit the Vatican, and occasionally enjoy an audience with the Pope. In 1984, from left to right, Srs. Mary Randal Sup, Maria Hertilde Spiegels, Mary Leanne Laney, Maria Hiltrude Gieske, and Maria Raphaelita Böckmann, superior general, meet with Pope John Paul II.

In 1983, Chardon hosted 87 sisters, five translators, and three secretaries for the International Congress on the Apostolate of the Sisters of Notre Dame. Shown here are presenters from India, Germany, the United States, Brazil, and England. In front of the American flag is superior general Sister Maria Raphaelita, who convened the congress to unify the congregation in the spirituality of ministry.

The Sisters of Notre Dame staffed Gesu School, University Heights, for 75 years. In 1966, enrollment peaked at 957 children. Sr. Mary Judith (St. Albert) Bucco is shown here with her second-graders in the early 1980s, part of the congregation's consistent ministry of preparing children for reception of the sacraments. Over the years, 12 young women from Gesu Parish became Sisters of Notre Dame. (GP.)

For 53 years, at Ansel Road and in Lyndhurst, Sr. Mary François Zappone (1923–2014) taught Julie Billiart School's primary students and prepared them for First Communion. Continued growth at Julie Billiart stretched capacity at the Arter mansion and resulted in moving the primary grades to Providence Hall at nearby Notre Dame College for 12 years. The school added a gymnasium in 1972 and a new classroom wing in 1979.

At Immaculate Heart of Mary School in Austintown, Ohio, the sisters on the faculty welcomed Sr. Margaret Mary Gilmore during a 1988 visit from Rome. Enjoying a light moment during that visit were Srs. Mary Corleen Trares, Caron Kehner, Sharone Matoney, Chrisara Fishley and Sharon (Donnalynn) Kovalcik. Immaculate Heart was a Notre Dame school from 1956 until 2012.

As fewer sisters were available, Catholic elementary schools hired more laymen and laywomen to share in the ministry of teaching. Srs. Mary Louismarie Nudo (front), Margaret (Lorenz) Hartman, Edana Perusek, and Ann Winchester were on staff at St. Joseph, Amherst in 1984. The sisters began teaching at St. Joseph in 1946, and they continue to serve on the parish staff in 2019.

Sr. Mary Carmelita Wagner gathers a primary reading group at St. John School in Warrenton, Virginia, in 1988. Sister Carmelita's first ministry was cooking, but, like many sisters, she changed ministries, and taught for 40 years in the primary grades. The sisters served in the parish elementary school and parish school of religion in Warrenton from 1968 to 1997.

In 1987, principals of St. Stephen, St. Boniface, and St. Michael Schools began planning to share resources to improve education for urban children. Supported by pastors and Cleveland's Bishop Anthony Pilla, "founding mothers" Srs. Regina (Glenda) Davala, Grace Mary (Foster) Corbett, Ann Winchester, and Virginia (Bruce) Reesing laid the foundations to ensure Metro Catholic School's strong beginning when it opened in 1988 with 766 children.

At St. Michael the Archangel in Canton, Ohio, Sr. Mary (Lauranne) Hunter worked with these children in 1988. The sisters staffed the school from 1953 until 2006, with a top enrollment of 638 children in 1967. Sisters also served as pastoral minister and as pastoral associate until 2013—a total of 60 years at St. Michael. In Stark County, the sisters also taught in Canal Fulton, Harrisburg, Massillon, and Maximo.

Sr. Mary Elizabeth (John Edwin) Daly engages her primary students at Metro Catholic in 1988. The Boniface Campus is home to preschool, kindergarten, and grade 1. At the St. Stephen Campus, grade 2–4 classes are held in the Michael Building, and grades 5–8 meet in the Stephen Building. Supporting Metro are the near-west parishes of St. Augustine, Barbara, Boniface, Colman, Michael, Stephen, and La Sagrada Familia.

The Sisters of Notre Dame have taught at Cardinal Gibbons High School in Raleigh, North Carolina, since 1972, when the sisters also accepted parish schools in Fayetteville and Burlington and Nazareth Children's Home, Raleigh. Sr. Janet Mary (Raphaelle) Schemmel taught chemistry and math and served as academic dean at the diocesan coeducational high school, where a new school on a larger campus opened in 1999.

Sr. Mary Catherine (Roy) Romancik works with an advanced French class at Regina High School in 1977. Study trips to France, Spain, England, and Germany were familiar events at Regina, Notre Dame Academy, and Notre Dame–Cathedral Latin, including a student exchange partnership with the Liebfrauenschule Vechta that brought German girls to study at Regina, Notre Dame, and Notre Dame–Cathedral Latin while Ohio girls studied in Vechta.

After 25 years as a boarding and day school, Notre Dame Academy, Middleburg, phased out its residence hall and admitted boys in 1990. Sr. Mary Laura Wingert, longtime Notre Dame Academy art teacher, enjoyed additional art lab space created in the former dorm rooms. The sisters stayed on staff in Middleburg until 2000. In 2009, the school became a nonsectarian independent school called Middleburg Academy.

In 1988, Notre Dame Academy merged its 110-year heritage with Cathedral Latin School's 63-year legacy to create Notre Dame–Cathedral Latin School, the only coeducational Catholic high school in Geauga County. Hundreds of people celebrated the dedication, including provincial superior Sr. Rita Mary Harwood, principal Sr. Donna Marie Paluf, Cleveland bishop Anthony Pilla (a Latin alumnus), and alumni moderator Br. Frank Nurthen, SM.

Sr. Rita Mary (Margarette) Harwood (center) was an elementary school teacher and principal, and community supervisor for elementary education, before serving as provincial superior from 1984 to 1993. Sr. Mary Immaculette Moose from California (left) and Sister Rita Mary joined Sr. Joan Marie Recker at a summer interprovince gathering in Toledo. Since 1995, Sister Rita Mary has been secretary for Parish Life and Development with the Diocese of Cleveland.

The National Congress on Our Apostolate, July 18–24, 1982, at Regina High School and Notre Dame College brought more than 1,100 sisters from all four US provinces to revitalize the apostolic mission and learn about their shared heritage. Through lectures, focus sessions, futuring, liturgies, and social hours, the sisters established cross-province relationships. Many sisters enjoyed bus tours to St. Peter, St. Joseph Cemetery, Mount St. Mary's, and Ansel Road.

On April 24, 1978, Mother Teresa of Calcutta visited Notre Dame College. She toured the buildings, visited with faculty and students of Notre Dame College and Julie Billiart School, and spoke at a luncheon in Connelly Center. Here, she is escorted by college president Sr. Mary Marthe Reinhard; Sister Mary Doris, MC; and Sr. Helene Marie (Therese Martin) Gregos, professor of education. (Larry P. Brown.)

Notre Dame College
4545 College Rd
Cleveland, Ohio 44121
fRM.

Missionaries of Charity
54A, Lower Circular Road,
CALCUTTA-16

10/6/78

Dear Sr. Mary Martha

Thank you for all your love - You shared and the care you took of me while with you.
Your people are so beautiful - the young faces so full of goodness & joy - I am praying much for your College. especially telling Our Lady - to make sure to make your College another Nazareth - where she can take care of the young students as she took care of Jesus. I have great faith in the "Memorare" tell Our Lady - it has never been heard - Pray for me   God bless you
                                        M Teresa mc

After the American visit and her return to Calcutta, Mother Teresa thanked Sister Mary Marthe and the college with this note.

Since 1962, the Notre Dame Guild's main work has been the annual Chicken Barbecue & Boutique. First held at the provincial center, the barbecue moved in 1965 to Notre Dame Academy, where for more than 50 years it has brought together thousands of families, friends, neighbors, and alumni. Here, guild moderator Sr. Donna Marie (Karena) Daniels and provincial superior Sr. Rita Mary Harwood promote the 1984 barbecue.

The Chicken Barbecue & Boutique has been a masterpiece of detailed planning and constant assessment. For decades, Sr. Margaret (Nathan) Hess and her colleagues in the community office, finance department, and mission advancement engineered advertising, purchasing, setup, logistics, and evaluation. One barbecue afternoon, Sister Margaret confers with Otto Hanish, longtime manager of buildings and grounds. Members of the Hanish family have worked at Notre Dame Education Center since 1963.

August Siemer tended the Green Road orchards and vineyards from 1925 to his death in 1983. For many years, he and his family lived in this white frame house, which had been called Notre Dame Heights when the sisters acquired the property in 1925. Siemer also purchased and delivered the weekly market order of fresh produce for the larger convents. (Joe Darwal and Sun Newspapers.)

From 1965 through 1999, the chickens were barbecued in cement-block charcoal pits on the hill behind Notre Dame Academy. Jack Wadowick is credited with perfecting the "secret" sauce, while Larry Divoky masterminded early barbecue operations. On the two 1991 barbecue Sundays, more than 14,000 dinners were served. Since 2000, Bar-B-Que Traveler has prepared the chicken and ribs.

Sr. Donna Marie (Loris) Paluf, Hamburger Hungry, and Sr. Mary Barbara (Bernadel) Knuff enjoy a 1972 Red Barn picnic at the provincial center. Red Barn coupons had been a thank-you to Geauga County blood donors; so many sisters donated blood that Red Barn brought the meals to the provincial center. Notre Dame Education Center still hosts Red Cross blood drives coordinated by Sr. Mary Kathleen Tobin.

Since 1885, thirty women from St. Joseph, Randolph, have become Sisters of Notre Dame. Some who gathered in Chardon in 1982 are, from left to right, (first row) Srs. Mary Ruth (Eymard) Koby, Dolora Horning, Damien May, Wilbert Koby, and Winfred Koerber; (second row) Srs. Corleen Trares, Doreen Strahler, Clareen Moledor, Barbara (Isidore) Klodt, Deotila Paulus, Caron Kehner, Verone Wohlwend, Dorotheus Wise, Merita Strahler, and Clementin Eichler.

When Sr. Mary Dorotheus Wise (1902–2007) was 89 years old, she agreed to work only part-time in the provincial center's main kitchen, specializing in the soup for the noon meal. She had served in food service since 1928, mostly at Notre Dame College and the Ansel Road and Chardon convents, always with great kindness and deep prayer. Her apple pies and embroidery were legendary and exquisite.

After teaching primary children for 16 years, Sr. Mary Wilfred Diederich (1909–1999) earned a nursing degree from St. Louis University and began serving the sisters' health needs in 1949. In the infirmary at Ansel Road, at Marian Hall, and in Chardon, Sister Wilfred was gracious, efficient, and droll. Here, Geauga physicians Neil Johnston, Oscar Oca, Arturo Dimaculangan, and Oscar Brinckmann celebrate her golden jubilee in 1979.

One response to the 1986 General Chapter call to be an active apostolic community sent to evangelize was the Gathering Days, an intense four-day experience of private and group prayer, discussion, and community-building. During 15 sessions at Bethany in 1988, diverse groups of 25 sisters explored aspects of renewal. Here, Srs. Margaret Mary (John Patrick) Friel and Mary Jean (Myles) Strathern enjoy a small-group session.

After Notre Dame Academy discontinued the boarding school, the barn-turned-dormitory was repurposed again as Bethany Retreat Center, where sisters, associates, and school and parish groups enjoy a quiet space for retreats and days of reflection. These sisters pray and sing at Bethany's dedication in 1981.

By 1991, the sisters could choose to wear a modified habit or simple clothing, with or without a veil. Welcoming a visitor, from left to right, Srs. Elizabeth Mary (Crucis) Biebelhausen, Mary St. Dominic Nudo, Frederic Hoover, Mary Ann (Timothee) Gemignani, and Merita Strahler illustrate a variety of clothing choices. All are wearing the congregational cross and ring as an outward sign of religious consecration.

Our House, a three-bedroom family home in Roaming Shores, Ashtabula County, was purchased in 1987. Since then, five more bedrooms have been added as well as a sunroom with three walls of windows. The house is well used all year, as groups of sisters spend a week, a weekend, or a quiet day at the lake. This group of retired sisters enjoy a summer day in 2006.

Many sisters continued as educators by transitioning from the classroom to religious education, including the parish school of religion, sacramental programs, and adult faith formation. Sr. Mary Charlita Slough (1923–2017) directed religious education and the Rite of Christian Initiation at St. Justin Martyr, Eastlake, from 1989 to 1997. Nurturing the faith life of God's people extended to companioning Jean Kiepper when she became an associate of Notre Dame.

The ministry of writing now engages a number of sisters. Besides serving as general editor of the *Christ Our Life* series for 13 years, Sr. Mary Kathleen (Kirene) Glavich (left) writes and edits books, blogs weekly at *Catholic Faith Corner*, and gives talks and retreats on spirituality and faith formation. Sr. Melannie Svoboda gives talks and retreats, and writes articles, spiritual books, and a weekly blog called *Sunflower Seeds*.

St. Julie Model Primary School in Buseesa, in Uganda's Hoima diocese, was begun by Notre Dame sisters from Thousand Oaks and Covington in 1995. Sr. Mary Annete Adams (right) joined the mission as a teacher in 1998 and helped develop Uganda's initial formation program. During three summer visits, Sr. Regina (Gerard) Alfonso provided teaching workshops for the lay faculty.

Notre Dame Skills Lab opened in 1995 in two Regina High School classrooms, providing one-on-one tutoring, high school credit recovery, and summer classes. Other sites were Cleveland Heights, Rocky River Drive, Bellaire-Puritas, and Chardon, until the 2011 move to SS. Robert and William Parish, Euclid, with Sr. Mary Carole (Marleene) Geiger as director. In 2000, the Skills Lab served 574 students in more than 4,800 hours of tutoring.

After a long career in secondary school teaching and administration, Sr. Mary Frances Murray earned a doctorate in higher education administration and served at Notre Dame College. She was named provincial superior in 1993. Elected to the general government in Rome in 1998, she served the international congregation for 12 years. Since returning to Chardon, Sister Mary Frances ministers once again at Notre Dame College.

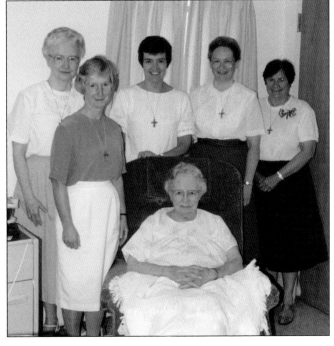

Former provincial superiors and newly installed Sr. Melannie Svoboda meet in the health care center in 1999 with Sr. Mary Elise Krantz (seated), who had served as provincial from 1961 to 1973. From left to right are Sr. Mary Jean (Ann Regina) Hoelke (1999), Sr. Rita Mary (Margarette) Harwood (1984–1993), Sister Melannie (1999–2005), Sr. Mary Frances Murray (1993–1998), and Sr. Mary Elizabeth Sakach (1983–1984).

Five

BECOMING ONE
2000–2019

As the 21st century begins, the Chardon Sisters of Notre Dame are experiencing major transitions centered on oneness and wholeness, with energy and deep peace.

Superior general Sister Mary Sujita urged the sisters to be on mission "to the nations," and Pope Francis has invited Christians to serve people "on the margins." The *Constitutions of the Congregation of the Sisters of Notre Dame* calls the sisters to be "impelled by a missionary spirit [to] respond to the needs of the times and share God's compassionate love with people of all faiths and cultures, particularly those who are poor and marginalized." Chardon sisters were missioned to the Philippines, Uganda, and Nicaragua, and renewed their commitment to urban Catholic schools on the margins closer to home.

Attuned to justice, peace, and the integrity of creation, the sisters formulated corporate stances opposing human trafficking and promoting clean water. Although they have withdrawn from 26 schools and 30 parishes since 1999—some of them after 30 to 100 years of ministry—the sisters continue to work in elementary, secondary, and higher education, especially taking responsibility for sponsorship, nurturing the charism, and working with lay colleagues to continue the legacy of Notre Dame educational excellence. In addition, new ministries extend the congregation's commitment to women and children.

To help people know themselves loved by God, sisters provide spiritual direction, pastoral visits, and prison ministry. They welcome associates of Notre Dame who participate more deeply in the sisters' prayer and ministries. Retreats, prayer groups, and faith sharing with one another, parishioners, and neighbors intensify the sisters' own spiritual growth.

Like other congregations, the sisters face the reality of fewer and older members: in 2018, Chardon had 270 sisters, down from 785 in 1965, with a median age of 75. Still, the mission is full of life, looking toward 2020 when the four US provinces reunite as a single unit. Through extensive committee work, a national novitiate, and national conferences on education and spirituality, the sisters are experiencing unity. Contemplative in spirit, prophetic in action, they continue the mission of transforming the world in God's image.

The congregation celebrated its sesquicentennial in 2000 with an international pilgrimage to the founding sites in Mülhausen, Coesfeld, and Namur. Sister Mary Sujita, elected superior general in 1998, called the sisters to renewal in the spirit of the founders. Here, Sr. Mary Joell Overman (superior general from 1986 to 1998) and Sr. Maria Raphaelita Böckmann (1974–1986) join Sister Mary Sujita beneath the ancient crucifix in St. Lambert Church, Coesfeld.

In recent years, sisters from all parts of the congregation have had the opportunity to make a prayerful pilgrimage of renewal to the sacred sites of congregational history: Namur, Coesfeld, Mülhausen, and Rome. In 2000, Srs. Mary Jeanine Stosik (first row, second from left) and Julie Rose Keck (second row, second from right) are welcomed by a group of German sisters.

Notre Dame in Cleveland returned to its roots in 2000 by inaugurating the Legacy Project, a literacy center housed at the former Ansel Road provincial center, redeveloped for senior housing and community resources. Sr. Mary Frances (Donald Ann) Dunham was the first director of the project, which provided instruction in reading, writing, math, science, and social studies as well as test preparation for GED candidates until 2017. (MA.)

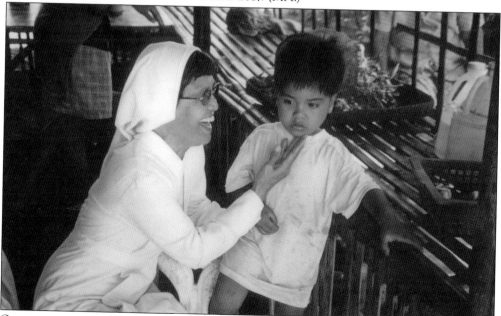

One sesquicentennial commitment of the congregation was a response to a request to establish a mission in the Philippines. Chardon's Sr. Mary Niño Ranes (1943–2017) and three Indonesian sisters moved to Sibunag on the island of Guimaras to live among the people and assess their needs. Soon, the sisters began formal and informal religious education; in 2004, they built a convent and kindergarten.

Sisters continue to fill various roles in parish elementary schools in addition to classroom teaching and administration. Some are library or classroom aides, tutors, and lunch supervisors. After 21 years as principal at St. Mary in Chardon, Sr. Sandra (Donnan) Nativio helps the technology teacher with this primary computer class in 2011. (MA.)

A National Blue Ribbon School of Excellence and a National Green Ribbon School, Metro Catholic School in Cleveland celebrated its 30th anniversary in 2018. Among its 520 students were children from 14 different countries on four continents, speaking six different languages; some were the children of refugees. Ethnically, the children were 30 percent Latino, 20 percent African/African American, 25 percent Caucasian, 20 percent mixed, and 5 percent Asian and Middle Eastern.

Julie Billiart Akron, near St. Sebastian Parish, opened in 2017 to children in primary grades, and added grades 3–5 in 2018. JB Akron is the first expansion school in the JB network, which is dedicated to meeting the needs of children with learning differences through small classes, individualized instruction, social learning, and additional on-site therapies. Here, kindergarten teacher Emily Sweeney instills a love of writing. (JB.)

When St. Francis School opened in 1887, Cleveland's East Seventy-First Street neighborhood was a German farming community. Houses and streets changed, and the parish closed in 2009, but the sisters and the school remain, supported by the Sisters of Notre Dame and the diocese, providing quality education in a caring environment where children learn to be peace-builders. Longtime principal Sr. Karen (Raymond) Somerville cultivates youth leadership. (MA.)

After World War II, the sisters taught at Mother of Sorrows School in Ashtabula for seven years. In 1997, Sisters of Notre Dame returned to Ashtabula County with parish ministries in Orwell (1997), Jefferson and Ashtabula (1998), Conneaut (2002), and Geneva (2003). In 2010, St. John School welcomed Sr. Maureen Burke as principal/president, beginning a new era of growth. Here, Sr. Sally Huston teaches math at St. John.

Cleveland Central Catholic High School's 2018 seniors had a 100 percent graduation rate and earned nearly $2 million in college scholarships. Counselors like Sr. Mary Josephe Fernandez have helped students match skills and interests with academic opportunities. Cleveland Central Catholic's original four-campus school was consolidated in 2003 at St. Stanislaus, where a major capital campaign and significant gifts have provided new classrooms, labs, athletic fields, a chapel, and an increased endowment. (MA.)

Declining enrollment forced Regina High School to close in 2010, but 30 seniors earned Regina diplomas and a year's worth of college credits as dual-enrollment students at Notre Dame College. Sara Bender, Megan Smith, Ellen Froliklong, Laura Moore, and Michelle Wilson sang at their 2011 graduation. Notre Dame College purchased the building and renovated to create classrooms, offices, nursing labs, and performance studios. (Jim Olexa and Sun Newspapers.)

Continuing the Notre Dame commitment to secondary education in the city, sisters continue to minister at Cleveland Central Catholic High School. Sr. Mary Karen (Marie Jude Andrew) Dolovacky, who has taught science at Central since 2011, was honored as the outstanding chemistry teacher of 2017 by the Cleveland Section of the American Chemical Society. Since 2013, ninety-eight percent of Central Catholic's seniors graduate, and eighty-five percent are accepted into colleges. (MA.)

Notre Dame Schools was established in 2016, uniting Notre Dame Elementary, led by principal Barbara Doering, and Notre Dame–Cathedral Latin under a single president and board of directors. When Notre Dame–Cathedral Latin earned the National Blue Ribbon School of Excellence award in 2018, principal Joseph Waler, teacher Maureen Wahl, president Dr. Michael Bates, and former president Sr. Jacquelyn (Evarista) Gusdane attended the Washington, DC, ceremony. (NDCL.)

Sisters have served in higher education at Notre Dame College since 1922, at Cleveland's St. John College (1928–1946), and at the Catholic University of America (1936–1969). In 2019, sisters are also on staff at Kent State University, Borromeo College, St. Mary Seminary and Graduate School of Theology, and Catholic Distance University. Sr. Carol (John Edward) Ziegler teaches the spirit and mission of Notre Dame College to these 2009 freshmen. (NDC.)

Sr. Melannie Svoboda was a high school English teacher and freelance writer before she became Chardon's novice director in 1982, and then a member of the formation team for the Jesuits' Chicago-Detroit Province. During Sister Melannie's term as provincial superior (1999–2005), Chardon launched the associate relationship and the mission effectiveness office, and completed a major expansion of the health care center. Sister Melannie continues to write and lead retreats.

Notre Dame College's first full-time male undergraduates began classes in 2001, bringing coeducation to the 79-year-old college. Within 10 years, enrollment had tripled, with a 50-50 balance of men and women. The college hired more full-time faculty, developed turf fields for soccer, lacrosse, rugby, and football, and added classroom space in the Regina building. Here, students David Nelson and Paul Kordich move into North Hall, one of two new dorms. (NDC.)

After the 2006 General Chapter, the sisters focused increased energy on ministries relating to justice, peace, and the integrity of creation. Sr. Kathleen Mary (Norah) Ryan worked for 30 years at the Cleveland diocese's Commission on Catholic Community Action, often engaging local Catholic high schools in activism and advocacy. Seen here with Rev. Gerald Bednar, Jerome Walcott, and Patrick Shea, Sister Kathleen presents a Faithful Citizenship workshop in 2008.

The Collaborative to End Human Trafficking began in 2007 when sisters from seven Greater Cleveland congregations, including Srs. Mary Barbara (John Kenneth) Daugherty; Toby Lardie, HM; and Laura Wingert committed their experience in education, health care, social services, and law to inform the public about human trafficking and to take action to free those caught in forced labor and commercial sex.

In conjunction with the United Nations' Decade for Water 2005–2015, the Chardon Province adopted a corporate stance, Water for Life, committing itself to prayer and personal and communal actions protecting and conserving fresh water, and supporting people's access to clean water. The Water for Life Committee sponsored public educational programs, like Sr. Alice (St. Benedict) Dugar's presentation at Notre Dame College in 2013. (NDC.)

In her ministry with the Renee Jones Empowerment Center, Sr. Cecilia (Ranata) Liberatore is a personal support advocate for women and girls who are victims of commercial sex trafficking. She is present in specialized human trafficking courts for adults and juveniles, and does individual visitations in the county jail and rehabilitation facilities. She participates in group sessions, street outreach, educational presentations, and interagency collaboration throughout Greater Cleveland. (MA.)

Prison ministry engages sisters in writing to prisoners and preparing small gifts for incarcerated women to give their children. Sr. Mary Dion Horrigan supports women in the Cuyahoga County Jail and Ohio prisons through visits and 12-step spirituality. More than 400 volunteers share the diocesan ministry to the incarcerated and their families established by Sr. Rita Mary Harwood, who accompanied the bishop for the county jail Christmas 2018 liturgy. (DC.)

From the congregation's beginning, the sisters have cared for children in homes for orphans and in schools. At Blessing House in Lorain, Sr. Mary (Marie Timothy) Berigan and her colleagues provide a calm, safe place for children to live while their parents resolve their issues. Sisters have also staffed Boys Hope Girls Hope in Garfield Heights (1999–2006), and, since 2013, House of Champions, an after-school home near Metro Catholic. (MA.)

At-risk children continue to be a focus in the sisters' work. In her ministry with the Cuyahoga County public defender, juvenile division, headed by attorney Sam Amata (left), Sr. Mary Margaret (Lorenz) Hartman works on cases involving delinquency and custody. Sister Margaret earned her law degree at the University of Akron School of Law through the university's Matthew 25:31–46 Scholarship for women religious who serve the poor. (MA.)

Like the Women's Hope Cooperative at Cleveland's St. Catherine Parish, directed by Sr. Mary Janeta Stamper from 1995 to 2004, the Women's Outreach Center in Cleveland offers women skill development and a sense of community leading to self-sufficiency. These participants and their children spent an afternoon with the sisters in Chardon, accompanied by Srs. Felicia Petruziello, CSJ; Lisette Petelin; and Patricia Gentile.

Backed by Food for the Poor and the American Nicaragua Foundation, four Sisters of Notre Dame settled at Sangre de Cristo Parish, Jinotega, Nicaragua, in 2008 to minister there and in nearly 30 mountain communities, teaching religion, English, sewing, gardening, sacramental preparation, and youth leadership. After nine years, Srs. Mary Charlotte Hobelman, Dolores Mikula, and Roseanna Mellert entrusted the mission to the Hermanas Inmaculatinas, a congregation from Mexico.

A novitiate for Notre Dame candidates from South Korea, Indonesia, Papua New Guinea, Vietnam, China, and the Philippines began in 2010 at Stella Maris Retreat Center in Bataan, Philippines, where Sr. Maresa Lilley (center) was the first novice director. In 2017, Srs. Marie Martina Nguyen (left) and Maria Emmanuel Vu professed perpetual vows in Vietnam. Supported by the Dan Meehan Foundation, Stella Maris is the Balanga diocese's first Catholic retreat center. (MA.)

Through Notre Dame Global Missions, Sr. Marie (Alice Patrick) Manning coordinates prayer, fundraising, and education of sisters and partners in mission about the sisters' work in India, East Africa, the Philippines, and Nicaragua, where Chardon sisters have served. ND Global Missions hosts visiting missionaries, provides speakers to many dioceses, sells mission crafts and fair trade products, and facilitates immersion trips and collaboration with Sisters of Notre Dame mission schools and women's empowerment projects. (MA.)

The Chardon Province's commitment to the mission in East Africa continued in the 21st century. Sr. Mary Therese (Joseph Paul) Dugan (center) spent two summers teaching scripture to the novices in Tanzania. Sr. Mary Annete Adams served in the formation house in Tanzania for 11 years, and continues as director of associates and secretary for the Holy Spirit delegation in East Africa, comprising Uganda, Tanzania, and Kenya.

From the days of the Art House on Ansel Road, the sisters have treasured the ministry of the visual arts. Sr. Megan Dull, shown creating the *Julie* statue in 1983, continues to use her gifts as a ceramic artist at TerraVista Studios. Other working visual artists include Sr. Laura Wingert, who also works in clay, and Sr. Maresa Lilley, who uses oil paint to proclaim God's goodness.

The emphasis on justice, peace, and the integrity of creation includes attention to the environment. A number of sisters volunteer in northern Ohio's extensive park systems, including Sr. Mary Julie Boehnlein (right), who has worked with the Geauga Park District since 2006, becoming an Ohio certified volunteer naturalist in 2009, and helping with park activities like making maple syrup each spring.

Continuing a rich tradition that began in the 19th century at the first convent on Superior Avenue, Sr. Mary Susan (Carlyn) Clark has given private piano lessons for years. Like her work as parish music director and high school music teacher, private music lessons allow her to lead students to a richer experience of life and of God's goodness. (MA.)

Nearly a dozen sisters are liturgical ministers in parishes around the province, in parish schools, and at Notre Dame Education Center. At St. Francis de Sales School, Parma, Sr. Mary Annette Therese Amendolia, parish liturgy director, leads the instrumental group and children's choir for a school liturgy in 2013.

Chaplaincy and pastoral care in hospitals, nursing homes, and hospice facilities are ministries in which more than 50 sisters have served. They pray with patients, bring the Eucharist, support families, educate about advance directives and end-of-life issues, and provide a comforting presence to and for colleagues. After teaching biology and religion, Sr. Mary Kendra Bottoms has served in pastoral care at St. John Medical Center in Westlake, Ohio, since 2004. (MA.)

With fewer priests available in many US dioceses, religious women have assumed parish leadership roles. In the Youngstown diocese, Sr. Regina Zeleznik was parish leader at St. Peter of the Fields, Rootstown, from 1995 to 1999, ministering alongside the canonical pastor and a permanent deacon. Sister Regina had been pastoral associate at St. Gabriel Parish in Greenville, North Carolina, and later served as director of pastoral outreach in Ohio's Columbiana County.

In 2011, Sr. Mary Susan (Avery) Wolf updated the Chardon Province about its new full-time technology department. The sisters' online engagement—the province website, blogs, and social media—supports mission and vocation awareness. The sisters often livestream community meetings. Sister Susan's Catholic Web Solutions internet ministry helps parishes create websites and social media content that advance their evangelizing mission.

Pastoral care at Cleveland's St. Francis Parish has been part of the mission of the sisters teaching in the school and in the parish school of religion, or CCD, since 1887. After two years as pastoral associate, Sr. Geraldine Marie (Bernerd) Tengler ministered as parish life coordinator from 2001 to 2009, working with the school faculty, coordinating liturgy and sacramental preparation, and gathering parishioners for prayer and celebrations. (DC.)

After long service in secondary education as teacher, principal, and president, including 24 years in Middleburg, Sr. Mary Cecilia (Ranata) Liberatore was ongoing formation director before being named provincial superior in 2005. During her six-year term, more sisters began to minister in social service agencies and spiritual and pastoral care. Chardon sisters were missioned to Nicaragua, Tanzania, and the Philippines, and collaborated with other women religious in the Cleveland diocese.

Sr. Mary Lucille Sennes (left) and chaplain Rev. Paul Sciarrotta join Sr. Mary Margaret Joseph Bobak in the health center dining room. As the health care center expanded and more nurses were needed, Sister Margaret Joseph (1952–2008) transitioned from teaching to nursing in 1990, serving as charge nurse from 2002 to 2008. Linda Hunt Pasek was director of nursing from 1990 to 1999, a position held by Caralyn Treharne since 2011.

Through their ministry with young adults, sisters provide spiritual mentoring, faith-based community living, service, and weekend retreats. The South Euclid discernment house provided a setting for Sr. Kathleen Mary Hine (left) to offer programming with young people like Kelley Rush and Theresa Lee. Since 2016, the Sisters of Charity Foundation has sponsored a Summer Fellows program matching young adult interns in nonprofit agencies with women religious mentors. (MA.)

Since its dedication in 2018, Notre Dame Village has become home to more than 100 people in cottage homes and independent-living apartments. Operated by Jennings, the Village offers an intergenerational experience linked with the activities of the pre-K–12 Notre Dame Schools, an invitation to share the liturgical and cultural life of the sisters in the provincial center, and involvement in the Geauga County community. (MA.)

At the national novitiate house in Covington, directors Sr. Marla Monahan (Covington), left, and Sr. Mary Rose Moser (Toledo), right, welcomed novices Mayra Martinez and Nicole Varnerin for their formative year in 2016. During the year, the novices studied scripture and the vows, helped in the provincial center's health care center, tutored children, and worked with social service ministries in Cincinnati. Sister Nicole professed first vows in Chardon in 2018.

The National Education Office (NEO) and the Education Advisory Council (EAC) work together to provide professional support, resources, and networking for 15 sponsored schools and centers and 21 affiliated elementary and high schools, helping them embody the SND educational vision and guiding principles. Marianist Fr. James Heft, NEO director Sr. Mary Frances (Bernette) Taymans, and EAC chair Dr. Laura Koehl met during the 2015 Education Summit in Dayton.

After years of prayerful preparation, the Chardon sisters invited a group of women and men to enter into associate relationship, culminating in the first associate covenants made in July 2001. Through personal and liturgical prayer, monthly faith sharing, and service, associates share the SND charism by witnessing God's goodness and provident love. Sr. Regina (Glenda) Davala, Pamela Waitinas, and Claudette Matero serve as codirectors of the Chardon associates.

The associate relationship has become an integral part of worldwide SND life. Associates and directors from England, Indonesia, Korea, Brazil, and the four US provinces gathered in Chardon for international meetings in 2006 and 2017. Also in 2017, over 200 US associates from across the nation held a three-day gathering of prayer, formation, and celebration.

Since their installation, the leadership team has devoted a great deal of time and energy to planning for SND-USA as well as nurturing the lives of the sisters in the Chardon Province. Shown here in 2011 are, from left to right, (first row) Srs. Sally Huston, Margaret Gorman, and Jeanette Brown; (second row) Srs. Patricia Garrahan and Carol Dikovitsky. Srs. Patricia Gentile and Maureen Spillane have since joined the team.

With fewer sisters in active ministries, religious communities are increasingly intentional about embodying their core mission with lay colleagues. Sr. Mary Valerie Sweeney is the chief mission leader at Jennings, a continuing care community in Greater Cleveland sponsored by the Sisters of the Holy Spirit. At Notre Dame College, Sr. Carol Ziegler is the chief mission officer.

SND Summer Service immersion invites students in the high schools where the sisters serve to experience SND charism and spirituality. During the 13th summer service week in June 2018, students from Cleveland Central Catholic, Clearwater Central Catholic, Notre Dame–Cathedral Latin, and Notre Dame College spent three days serving children, homeless people, and refugees in Cleveland, and sharing prayer, reflection, games, and community with Sr. Lisa Novak and team. (MA.)

Mission effectiveness coordinator Sr. Lisa Novak shares the SND mission with employees of Notre Dame–linked institutions. The three-day Charism Experience at Bethany Retreat Center provides shared immersion in SND spirituality for small groups, particularly school staffs. Participants in 2007 were Cardinal Gibbons High School, Raleigh; Clearwater Central Catholic, Florida; Notre Dame Academy, Middleburg; Cleveland Central Catholic; Julie Billiart School; Notre Dame–Cathedral Latin; Regina; Notre Dame College; and Notre Dame Elementary.

Over 400 sisters from the four US provinces met in Columbus, Ohio, in July 2015 to pray, share, and celebrate a shared future as SND-USA. Some sessions focused on specific ministries, but the underlying purpose was for the sisters to get to know one another. During a break, Srs. Marie Alex Justavich and Mary Sherly Kodiyan got a warm Toledo hug from Sr. Celine Mary Bundschuh.

The eight-year process of "becoming one" was shepherded by superior general Sr. Mary Kristin Battles (center) and the four US provincial superiors—from left to right, Srs. Mary Anncarla Costello of Thousand Oaks, Delores Gatliff of Toledo, Ethel Parrott of Covington, and Margaret Gorman of Chardon, shown at the 2015 National Gathering. Here, the story of the Cleveland/Chardon Province ends, but the story of SND-USA continues, in God's provident care.

BIBLIOGRAPHY

Arntz, Sr. Mary Luke. *Three Memoirs: Sister Mary Odila, S.N.D., Sister Mary Bertilda, S.N.D., Sister Mary Fortunata, S.N.D.* Vol. VI, *In Our Lady's Household.* Chardon, OH: Sisters of Notre Dame, 1991.

Böckmann, Sr. Maria Raphaelita, and Sr. Maria Birgitta Morthorst. *History of the Congregation of the Sisters of Notre Dame of Coesfeld, Germany, 1900–1925.* Part One, Fifth Series. Trans. Sr. Mary Sarah Braun. Rome: Sisters of Notre Dame, 1997, 2000.

"Growth and Activity of the Congregation of the Sisters of Notre Dame." Unpublished manuscript. Cleveland, OH: 1938.

Hearts as Wide as the World: History of the Congregation of the Sisters of Notre Dame of Coesfeld, Germany—Mary Immaculate Province, Toledo, Ohio, 1924–2014. 2 vols. Toledo, OH: Sisters of Notre Dame, 2014.

Karlinger, Sr. Mary Jessica. "History of the U.S. Provinces." Unpublished manuscript. Chardon, OH: 2018.

Klein, Sr. Mary Vincentia. *Their Quiet Tread: Growth and Spirit of The Congregation of the Sisters of Notre Dame through Its First One Hundred Years, 1850–1950.* Catholic Life Publications. Milwaukee, WI: Bruce Publishing, 1955.

Pastva, Sr. Mary Loretta. *The Second 50 Years of the Coesfeld Sisters of Notre Dame. Cleveland/Chardon, Ohio, Province 1924–1975.* 2 vols. Chardon, OH: Sisters of Notre Dame, 2013.

Sisters of Notre Dame. *A Community of Faith: Notre Dame.* Chardon, OH: Sisters of Notre Dame, 1982.

Wittenburg, Sr. Mary Joanne. *Spreading the Fire: The Story of the Sisters of Notre Dame in California, 1924–2010.* Los Angeles, CA: Sisters of Notre Dame, 2012.

Discover Thousands of Local History Books
Featuring Millions of Vintage Images

Arcadia Publishing, the leading local history publisher in the United States, is committed to making history accessible and meaningful through publishing books that celebrate and preserve the heritage of America's people and places.

Find more books like this at
www.arcadiapublishing.com

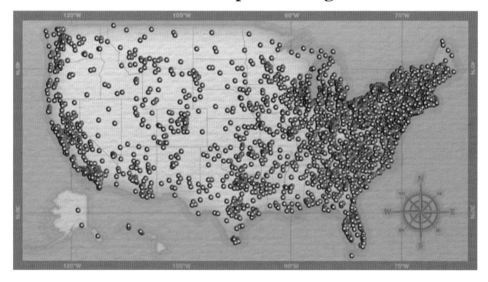

Search for your hometown history, your old stomping grounds, and even your favorite sports team.